It's the Walk,
Not the Talk

Six Points of Real Spirituality

LaFayette Scales

Destiny Image® Publishers, Inc.
P.O. Box 310
Shippensburg, PA 17257-0310

"Speaking to the Purposes of God for This Generation
and for the Generations to Come"

ISBN 1-56043-170-9

First Printing: 1997   Second Printing: 1998

For Worldwide Distribution
Printed in the U.S.A.

This book and all other Destiny Image, Revival Press,
and Treasure House books are available
at Christian bookstores and distributors worldwide.

For a U.S. bookstore nearest you, call **1-800-722-6774**.
For more information on foreign distributors,
call **717-532-3040**.
Or reach us on the Internet: **http://www.reapernet.com**

Contents

Chapter 1

Maturity Comes Through the Eye of the Beholder

But we all, with open face beholding as in a glass the glory of the Lord, are changed into the same image from glory to glory, even as by the Spirit of the Lord (2 Corinthians 3:18).

Paul told the Corinthians that we are all being changed into the Lord's image from "glory to glory" *as we behold the glory of the Lord as in a glass*. You are changed into what you behold. You become like that which you worship.

Psalm 115 speaks of the idols made by men who "...have mouths, but they speak not: eyes have they, but they see not: they have ears, but they hear not" (Ps. 115:5-6a). The Psalmist concluded, "They that make them are like unto them..." (Ps. 115:8). You become like that which you worship.

As You Behold Him

You are changed into what you behold. You are not changed into the Lord's image by the church you attend or the songs you sing. You're not changed just because you read your Bible or quote Scripture. You are not even changed because you pray, despite popular expression that says, "Prayer changes things." Prayer *can* change things, but you are not changed into His image just because you pray. Although all these things are necessary and good, Paul says we are changed into the image of the Lord *as we behold Him.* It is possible to read the Bible, sing, pray, go to the right church, and do all the right things, yet still not be changed into the Lord's image. But *to the degree that you behold Him* in your prayer, in the Word, and in your corporate church life, you will be changed. You are only changed as you behold Him.

You have to behold Him as Savior to be changed from a sinner to a saint. When you were healed by Jesus, you had to behold Him as your Healer to be changed into His image of wholeness. You moved from sickness to health as you beheld His face. The only way you can be delivered is to behold Him as Deliverer. Therefore the image you have of God can limit or initiate the amount of change in your life.

Changed Into His Image

Do you want to be more loving? Behold Jesus as a lover. You can't love until you behold Him as Love. But when you behold Him as Love and the Lover of your soul, you will be changed into that same image. As you behold Jesus, you will be changed from glory to glory by the Spirit of the Lord.

You can study the Scriptures and quote the Bible backward and forward, and still be a liar, a fornicator, and every other kind of sinner. However, when you behold Him, you will be changed. Whether you read through the New Testament and behold Him; or worship Him and behold Him, you cannot walk away from that encounter the same!

I look for Jesus Christ every time I enter into corporate worship. I want to know one thing: Where is He in our songs, in our prayer, and in our praise? If I can find Him, I know I am being changed. If I can't find Him, I know I will go away from that experience the same. I must behold Him in my worship, in the Word, and in my prayers. I must behold Him in the church. I must behold Him in my brothers and sisters. To the degree that I behold Him, I am changed, and no further.

John wrote, "Beloved, now we are the sons of God, and it doth not yet appear what we shall be: but we know that, *when He shall appear*, we shall *be like Him*; for we shall *see Him like He is* (1 Jn. 3:2). This apostle is saying that one day you will see Jesus fully. What will happen then? When He appears, you will *behold Him* in all His fullness, and you will *be fully changed.*

Maturation is the process of being *changed* from glory to glory, of moving forward from one spiritual level to another. However, every step up to a new spiritual level is really just reaching a higher level of the knowledge (the inner knowing) of God. Some people think rising to higher spiritual levels means you "talk in tongues" more, do more "spiritual" things or service, or get more Bible education. In fact, some people will accuse you of not "walking in the Spirit" if you're not involved in a lot of church activities.

Activity Isn't Necessarily Intimacy

Extreme levels of activity may actually be a sign of "outer court" experiences. There were three courts or areas in the

Tabernacle of Moses, and later in the temples built by Solomon and Herod. In every case, however, it's interesting to see that the closer you get to the innermost courts, the less activity you would see. For example, there was a lot of activity in the outer court. This was where large numbers of priests and Levites were busy slaying sacrificial animals. Animals were crying. Blood was flowing. Smoke was rising up. The fire on the altar was blazing. And meat was roasting on that great flame. Add to that the cries and petitions of the people who were hoping that their sacrifices would be accepted and the continual washings and other ritual activities of the priests. In sum, the outer court was a place of almost constant noise and activity.

The inner court (also called the "Holy Place") was a little more exclusive with a little less outward activity. Yet more internal things occured there. The priests who ministered in the inner court knew they had to judge themselves. They weren't looking for the ministry of those on the outside. Their thoughts were more focused: *I have to judge myself first, so I can then minister to God on behalf of the people. Then I can visit the Table of Shewbread and eat the bread reserved for the priests, smell the incense, and see the light from the golden candlestick.*

The final innermost court, the Most Holy Place, or Holy of Holies, was the most exclusive of all earthly places. This is where you had to go beyond the veil of the inner court to enter directly into God's presence. If you brought unrepented sin to that place, you would die with it right where you stood. Some of the incense from the inner court flowed in behind the veil with you as you came to stand one-on-one before God and behold His glory above the Mercy Seat of the Ark of the Covenant. This place was so exclusive that only one, or at most a handful of people, ever entered this place in a lifetime.

Many people choose to stay in the outer court bustling with religious activity, and they never really push into the things of the Spirit. Somehow we *still* call this kind of activity "spiritual ministry." (I wonder what God calls it?) A lot of activity might be the sign of a penalized priesthood that has been relegated to the outer court where the ministry for and to the people took place. Most of the people of the outer court were never permitted to come to the inner court and minister to God. In the days of Ezekiel, an entire priesthood was penalized for idolatry. Because they had worshiped idols, they were never allowed to enter the inner court or the innermost court again (Ezek. 44:10-14). People of the outer court can be marked by statements like, "I've been so busy working for the Master. I keep so busy serving my Jesus." Many songs of victory with no signs of change may be the fruits of a "penalized priesthood."

In contrast to a penalized priesthood, the sons of Zadok kept the priesthood pure when the rest of Israel went astray. God rewarded them by allowing them to continue to come near to minister directly to Him (Ezek. 44:15-16). They were able to go past the external activities of the outer court to minister in the presence of God.

Six Levels of Spiritual Maturity

Draw a horizontal line across on a piece of paper. Now draw six "steps" rising up from that horizontal line. Each of these six steps represents a level of spiritual maturity, and six is the number of man. Everything below the horizontal line is the "sub-Christian life." There are no steps below that line, for that is the realm of sinners, reprobates, and blasphemers. We all lived below this line before we received Jesus Christ as Lord and Savior.

Now on the first step above the line you've drawn, write "babes." On the second step write, "children." On the third step write, "young men." On the fourth step write, "fathers." On the fifth step write, "perfect man," and on the sixth step, write, "Glorified Man." These are the six steps of spiritual maturity described in the New Testament.

Let's begin our examination of these six steps.

Babes

When you come into the Kingdom of God, you enter the abundant life as a *babe*. What is a spiritual babe?

Wherefore laying aside all malice, and all guile, and hypocrisies, and envies, and all evil speakings, as new-born babes, desire the sincere milk of the word, that ye may grow thereby: if so be ye have tasted that the Lord is gracious (1 Peter 2:1-3).

A spiritual "babe" desires the sincere milk of God's Word. The writer of the Book of Hebrews said, "...ye have need that one teach you again which be the first principles of the oracles of God" (Heb. 5:12a). This passage refers to believers who should have matured beyond the "babe" stage, but had not. It also reveals what babes need, someone to teach them the first principles of the oracles of God. They are "such as have need of milk." Babes desire the sincere milk—or the first principles—of the oracles of God, not strong meat.

Hebrews 5:13 says, "...everyone that useth milk is unskil-ful...." Are they unskillful in spiritual things? No. They are unskillful in the *"word of righteousness."* Anyone who is un-skillful in the Word of righteousness is still a babe feeding on the first principles of the Christian life. That is not a negative statement! We must all come through this level in the spirit, just as we each came through it in the natural. New levels of maturity come in order, and one at a time. First you go to step one, learn the lessons there, and then you move up to the next level.

The writer of Hebrews tells us that "strong meat" is re-served for those who are of "full age." There is a clear differ-ence between babes, children and young men, and those who are in the "full age" stages. These include "fathers," the "per-fect man," and the "Glorified Man." The Bible says, "But strong meat belongeth to them that are full of age, even those who *by reason of use* have their *senses* [touch, smell, sight, hear, taste; the senses and emotions] exercised to discern both good and evil" (Heb. 5:14). As long as we're still getting hurt feelings we know we have not moved on to "strong meat," because we haven't trained our senses.

This "Nose Ring" Is for You

As long as the devil can operate in our lives in the sense realm, he will stick a "sense ring" through your nose and drag you by your senses all over the planet! You will drop out of church every week because somebody didn't speak to you, or because the leadership didn't let you prophesy, or sing, or dance. You will be offended because somebody didn't recog-nize you. That is what life is like under the bondage of un-trained and undisciplined senses. But God's Word says you can *train your senses*.

There are no shortcuts for this training; it only comes "by reason of use" (Heb. 5:14). By the "use" of what? The Word of God. You must begin to use God's Word and allow it to dictate your response to evil, to offense, and to persecution. Jesus told His disciples:

> *Blessed are they which are persecuted for righteous-*
> *ness' sake: for theirs is the kingdom of heaven. Blessed*
> *are ye, when men shall revile you, and persecute you,*
> *and shall say all manner of evil against you falsely, for*
> *My sake. Rejoice, and be exceeding glad: for great is*
> *your reward in heaven: for so persecuted they the*
> *prophets which were before you* (Matthew 5:10-12).

It takes training to mature our senses. What does this training do to our senses? It gives our senses the ability to *discern*, which means "to sift and sort, and distinguish" what is the divine emphasis of God's wisdom. Insight is discernment. Discretion is discernment. What do we discern? Good and evil. Strong meat is not deeper revelation; it is the ability to apply in practical ways the revelations you have received.

Jesus said, "My meat is *to do* the will of Him that sent Me, and to finish His work" (Jn. 4:34). Do you want to get to the "strong meat" of God? You don't have to get super spiritual and hunt for a "deeper" revelation. The meat of the Word is not simply "more knowledge." We discover the *meat* of God when we put feet on our faith and *do what God tells us to do*! Jesus said, "My meat is *to do* the will of Him that sent Me."

I'm not really impressed by most of the things people say. I've learned that if I want to move on to the meat of God's Word, then I need to go out and *do* the thing God has spoken to my inner being. James put it bluntly, "But be ye doers of the word, and not hearers only, deceiving your own selves" (Jas. 1:22).

People who drink spiritual "milk" are unskillful in the Word of righteousness. In other words, they'll say "amen" to everything, but then they won't apply any of it to their lives. They are "babes." God wants to bring us to maturity, to the point where we can receive the "strong meat" of His Word, and His will is *done* through our lives on earth as it is in Heaven.

Stretched Beyond Experience

Even in the "babe" stage of our spiritual walk, it is normal to stretch beyond our experience to a new revelation of God. I preach a lot of things that are beyond my present experience, but I know the time will come when I will be required to apply those truths in my life. The day will come when some circumstance will arise and I'll say, "Lord, what is this?" He'll respond, "Do you remember the revelation I had you preach about three months ago? It is time to walk in it"

Some people won't preach anything until they've "walked in it." I have a problem with this, even though it sounds good. You will never preach on hell if you wait to "walk in it." You'll never have a chance to preach on Heaven either. Does that mean you can never preach on adultery unless you've committed it? I've learned that when God gives me a revelation, it is truth, whether I've experienced it or not. I am obligated to preach it in the timing and the season God's requires. Down the line sometime, I will come to another intersection of time where I will be able to apply the truth of God's revelation to my life. My meat is *to do* the will of Him that sent me.

Oh, That Was Deep!

A lot of people jump, sing, shout, dance, and run the aisles. But after they buy all the tapes of other saints, saying, "Oh, that was deep," and after their feet hit the ground again, that is when I will find out what spiritual level they are on. Babies are essentially self-centered because their chief aim in life, their main cry, is: "We want to be fed, we want to be fed!" This isn't wrong as long as they move on to the "doing" stage at the right time. They're ignorant of the fact that they are held accountable for every truth that comes their way.

You know you have a real newborn babe in the Kingdom of God when his or her continual cry is, "Feed me. Teach me the oracles of Christ. Teach me the first principles of the things of God." These first principles include repentance from dead works, faith toward God, the doctrine of baptisms (plural), laying on of hands, the resurrection of the dead, and eternal judgment (see Heb. 6:1-2).

Sometimes I will teach the first principles in meetings and churches, and afterward, some people will nearly always come up to me and say "Oh, that's deep. That's heavy!" I have to tell them, "Man, that's milk. Those are first principles."

Little Children

God expects us to make measurable progress in a reasonable time. The second step of spiritual maturity is the level of "little children." Who are these children? John describes three levels of spiritual maturity in his first Epistle:

I write unto you, little children, because your sins are forgiven you for His name's sake. I write unto you, fathers, because ye have known Him that is from the beginning. I write unto you, young men, because ye have overcome the wicked one. I write unto you, little children, because ye have known the Father (1 John 2:12-13).

John is writing to "little children" at the beginning of this passage. These people aren't spiritual babes anymore; they are toddlers. These persons are beginning to seek more than just the sincere milk of the Word. They are beginning to be a little more skillful with the Word of righteousness. They are just beginning to go beyond the first principles of the oracles of God.

At the "child" stage, you know your sins have been forgiven for His name's sake. You also know that God has dealt finally with sin, even generational sin. You know that since your sins have been forgiven, you also have a right to respond and expect healing to come to your physical body ("...by whose stripes ye were healed" [1 Pet. 2:24]).

Sin brings death, disease, and mental torment. All these things will bring depression and confusion and cause you to want to quit in despair. They all lodge in the mind. When your sins are forgiven and you know it, you begin to develop a certain immunity to those kinds of things. You respond to them by saying, "That's not mine. I don't have to receive that because God says so."

When I used to deliver packages for United Parcel Service, people would say, "Oh, are those packages for me?" I would say, "You have to sign for them first." If they didn't sign for the boxes, they didn't get them. God showed me that the devil knocks at our door all the time with *all kinds* of packages. God said, "You need to know what to sign for." That truth is learned on the child level. I learned not to sign for sickness and disease, depression, confusion, or despair. A "child" has learned that his sins are forgiven him and that there are certain issues that are not his.

Get a Revelation of the Father

On the "child" level, you begin to understand that you are your Father's child. You begin to get a revelation of the Father. You begin to understand that you have stepped out of your generational, natural family. Now you are identified with the family of God. You begin to learn to know your sisters and brothers, your siblings in God's family. If a Muslim comes up to you and says, "Hey, brother," you'll tell him real quickly, "I'm not your brother." When you cross the street or campus and somebody says, "Hey brother, hey man," you'll say, "I'm not your brother because I know my Daddy. I know that my brothers and sisters who are part of His family— and you aren't part of it."

Now I know that disturbs some people's theology, but when you break into the "child" level, you will find that you're not related as "family" because of the color of your skin, your nationality, or your heritage. You are connected to God's family because of the Spirit of God. You are related to the family of God through a common bloodline through the Spirit; it's through the blood of the lamb.

We learn on the "child" level that we are not to relate to each other "after the flesh" anymore, but after the Spirit

(2 Cor. 5:16). These are the lessons learned by children. As long as I relate to you on the fleshly level, I'll always relate to you on a lower level than God expects me to relate to you. When Jesus went home, all that the people in that village could say was, "Wasn't this Mary's baby?" The Bible says, "And He did not many mighty works there because of their unbelief" (Mt. 13:58). The people had a *fleshly revelation* of who Jesus was, so they couldn't receive an impartation or revelation from Him.

Young Men

"I write unto you, young men, because ye have overcome the wicked one" (1 Jn. 2:13b). The "young man" level is marked by an ability to recognize and deal with the devil. Those at this level understand who they are, and they know their sins are forgiven. They still have a sincere desire for the milk of the Word, and though they are still fairly unskillful with the Word of righteousness, they are eating and drinking the Word voraciously. They grab every tape and book they can get their hands on. That's not a negative; it is necessary.

If you are in the "young man" stage of your spiritual development, you are beginning to *apply* what you've learned from all of those tapes, classes, books, and sermons. You have already identified your family members, and you've discovered that even though you can choose your friends, you are "stuck" with your relatives in God's family.

It is at this stage that you begin to deal with the devil and *overcome* him. You have identified your enemy, and you understand that your adversary is not flesh and blood. You have begun to understand that you are dealing with spirits, principalities, powers, spiritual wickedness, and rulers of darkness (Eph. 6:12). Perhaps you've started to notice that fewer people in your "family" have reached this stage—they're still fighting people instead of spirits! Jesus battled spirits, not people. He warned Peter that satan wanted to "sift" him like wheat (Jesus knew Peter would deny Him three times). But He looked beyond Peter's weakness, betrayal, and failure, and told him that He had already taken care of the problem.

And the Lord said, Simon, Simon, behold, Satan hath desired to have you, that he may sift you as wheat: But I have prayed for thee, that thy faith fail not: and when thou art converted, strengthen thy brethren (Luke 22:31-32).

Jesus interceded for Peter and the disciples instead of merely condemning them for their cowardice. He looked past the people to the devil behind the scheme. Jesus dealt with the problem in the spirit realm. He was letting Peter know, "I'm dealing with the 'young man' in you."

People at the "young man" level are mainly concerned with demonic activity. They want to know nine key things: (1) Who is the enemy? (2) What does the enemy have? (3) What can the enemy do? (4) Who is God? (5) What does God have? (6) What can God do? (7) Who am I? (8) What do I have? and (9) What can I do? Once you have learned those lessons in the "young man" stage, God will call you up to the next level.

Some Christians are afraid of demonic activity, but the truth is that once you know who they are, what they have, and what they can do, you won't be afraid anymore! All demons can do is manifest themselves in someone. Once you understand that these "manifestations" are just an act to make you afraid, you'll tread where the brave dare not go! You'll say, "What's a little demon?" At my "young man" level, I learned what demons are and what they can do. I found out who God is and what He can do. I found out who I was, what I had, and what I could do.

I Command Every Demon...!

When people come to me in fear about demons in their house, I just walk through the house opening up all the doors, windows, cabinets, and closets. Then I stand in the middle of the house and say, "In the name of Jesus, I command every demon from the top of the roof to the foundation of the house, from the north property line of this house to the south property line of this house, from the west property line of this house to the east property line of the house—I command you to go and not come back again. Now I welcome the Spirit of God into this place." Then I grab my hat and coat.

The people may say, "Is that all you're going to do? You're not going to anoint any doorknobs?" I just tell them, "No, I don't think all that's necessary because I know who He is, what He has, and what He can do. I found out who I am, what I have, and what I can do. What I have is the name of Jesus. I found out that demons tremble at the sound of His name and that they have to obey when we use His name." So not only do I get demons trembling, but I get them doing something! God's Word says, "In My name you shall cast out demons" (see Mk. 16:17), so I don't waste time carrying on long conversations with them! Their captain is the father of lies, so why would I want to talk to a liar? I just cast them out, put my hat and coat, and leave.

Smith Wigglesworth said one night he woke up and saw the devil sitting on the end of his bed. He just looked up, saw that it was the devil, and said, "Oh, it's just you." Then he rolled over and went back to sleep—totally ignoring his powerless guest. That was a man who knew who the devil was, what the devil had, and what the devil could do. He knew who God was, what God had, and what God could do. He also had found out who he was, what he had, and what he could do.

Don't let any devil give you trouble. Trust the words of Jesus: "Behold, I give unto you power to tread on serpents and scorpions, and over all the power of the enemy: and nothing shall by any means hurt you" (Lk. 10:19). Don't think that somebody has to be "special" to deal with the devil. It is just a sign that they have broken into that "young man" stage.

Fathers

"I write unto you, fathers, because ye have known Him that is from the beginning..." (1 Jn. 2:13a). Fathers in the faith are those who have passed through the levels of "babes," "little children," and "young men," to enter that stage where they begin to understand the eternal purposes of God.

These purposes are found in the Books of Romans and Ephesians (as well as throughout the Word of God). The fifth chapter of the Book of Romans gives us a promise. The sixth chapter of Romans gives us a principle. The seventh chapter of Romans gives us a problem or challenge, and the eighth chapter of Romans is where God's provision comes in.

This is God's *promise*: "Therefore being *justified* by faith, we have peace with God through our Lord Jesus Christ." (Rom. 5:1). The rest of Romans 5 deals with our justification in Christ Jesus. Romans 6 tells us that we must die with Christ in order to apply the promise of justification. You won't break into any other level unless you first die to your flesh. Romans chapter seven describes our *problem*—our *struggle* with the flesh and the law. This is what works death in us. Sometimes God slays the very thing that you *thought you knew* so He can give you a clearer revelation of it. This is the struggle between the law God is writing in your heart and your flesh and emotions. Yet this process leads to His *provision* for the problem in Romans 8, "There is therefore now *no condemnation...*" (Rom. 8:1). There is no guilt coming upon you.

"Fathers" know the eternal purposes of God, and they are ready to take responsibility for God's heritage. A father in the faith is one whom God is able to entrust with His heritage, His inheritance "in the saints" (see Eph. 1:18). Fathers understand that their inheritance is not a new car, a new house, or nicer clothes. Their inheritance is not in new buildings or seeing their names up in lights. Their inheritance is *in the saints*. If you want to know what the treasure of God is, just look at your brothers and sisters in the Lord. The treasure of God is on your right and on your left in the Body. Fathers understand what is valuable and what is not.

Where the True Riches Are

A lot of people run around calling me apostle, bishop, and all kinds of lofty titles and things. That's not necessary. The inheritance of God is in the saints. That is where the riches are. A father understands that, and he is willing to take responsibility for those riches. What's more, God is willing to give him that responsibility! In fact, Jesus said, "If therefore ye have not been faithful in the unrighteous mammon, who will commit to your trust the true riches?" (Lk. 16:11)

To Jesus, true riches were never "money." We shout when somebody gets a financial blessing, but God has a totally different definition for "true riches." How do you receive true riches? You must move into the fatherhood stage.

Paul wrote to the church at Corinth, "For though ye have ten thousand instructors in Christ, yet have ye not many fathers: for in Christ Jesus I have begotten you through the gospel" (1 Cor. 4:15). He wrote to Timothy, "Thou therefore, my son, be strong in the grace that is in Christ Jesus" (2 Tim. 2:1). All through the Bible, the anointing always flowed from father to son. The anointing flows from a father down to his sons just as Aaron's calling as priest flowed to his sons and to his sons' sons (1 Chron. 23:13). Elijah became a father figure to Elisha; when Elijah ascended up, Elisha said, "My father, my father!" (2 Kings 2:12)

Fathers take responsibility for God's heritage because they have learned the eternal purposes of God. God has used Dr. Myles Munroe to bring the Church into an awareness that God is a God of purpose and that there is an *original intent* of God. Fathers in the faith are people who understand that God had a plan long before there were any of the things we see today.

Paul declared that a great mystery was being revealed to the saints: "Christ in you, the hope of glory" (Col. 1:27b).

Christ, the hope of glory, has come and tabernacled inside your house. He wants to live out His kingly principles through you. God has wrapped Himself in you! You are a sermon preached, and you are to eat the heavenly Manna and then become *living manna* for other people. Paul told the Corinthians, "Ye are our epistle written in our hearts, known and read of all men" (2 Cor. 3:2). Until you understand this principle, you can't be a father. That is where He wants to take you. He wants you to be a father or mother to His heritage.

The final two levels of spiritual maturity, the "perfect man" and the "Glorified Man," are entirely different from the four levels we have already discussed. They are achieved through the *unity of the Body*, rather than through individual obedience, and they can only be achieved as we each obediently pass through the first four levels of spiritual maturity in Christ.

Chapter 2

We Have to
Press in Together

God's maturing work in "babes," or new believers, is an *individual* work. The same is true of His dealings with believers at the "little children" level, the "young men" level, and even the "fathers" level. God uses mature believers and anointed leaders to bring instruction and guidance to new believers, but the progress of each individual depends almost totally on his or her personal response to God. The Holy Spirit works in you personally to help you experience individual breakthroughs, yet there are even higher levels of maturity that can only be achieved as a part of an obedient *corporate* body!

Yet I have to emphasize that God is a God of order. First, you have to see what God's plans are, of course. That is why the "father" phase or step is so important. It is in this step that you learn to discern God's intent in your situation. This keeps you from speaking against and getting frustrated with "what you see." Once you consider what God has said and stop looking at the natural, temporal things you see, you will then begin to move up to the next level.

The Seen and the Unseen Realms

Babes, children, and young men (or young women) will always be dealing primarily with "what they see." It is in the "father" level that God moves you beyond the "seen realm" into the realm of the Spirit where you are caught up into His presence. In a sense, you will become like John on the Isle of Patmos when he was shown the mystery of the seven stars or churches. He saw that some were polluted, others were persecuted, one was lukewarm, and another had a Jezebel who was teaching and seducing the people (Rev. 1:1-20).

God will tell you just as He told John, "Come up hither, and let Me *show you things to come*" (see Rev. 4:1). When John went up to the higher level, he could see the elders offering worship to God and to the Lamb of God. He saw the scroll of God and watched as the seals of judgment were broken. He saw that a victory was coming, and he could see the travail the earth would have to endure to bring forth the manifested sons of God. (The tribulation and everything else described between Revelation chapters 5 and 19 are just the birthing pains necessary to bring forth the sons of God.)

"And from the days of John the Baptist until now the kingdom of heaven suffereth violence, and the violent take it by force" (Mt. 11:12). Up until now, the Kingdom of God has suffered from the assaults of the enemy, but now it is time for us to do the assaulting! Fathers in the Kingdom are violent, and they take the Kingdom through the force of intercession and fervent prayer. This in turn helps prepare the many-membered Body of Christ to ascend to the next step of maturity in God's Kingdom.

The Perfect Man

*Till we all come into the unity of the faith, and of the knowledge of the Son of God, **unto a perfect man,** unto the measure of the stature of the fulness of Christ: that we henceforth be no more children, tossed to and fro, and carried about with every wind of doctrine...* (Ephesians 4:13).

After you have reached the "father" stage in your individual walk with God, there is only one direction to go—upward! The Lord wants to take you on up to the level of the "perfect man" that Paul described in his letter to the Ephesians. Notice his wording at the beginning of Ephesians 4:13: "Till we *all...." This sixth level, the level of the "perfect man," can only be achieved by moving from "me" to "we"!*

Paul is saying that you can become a "perfect man" only when you join your brethren and "*you all*" come into the unity of the faith in the knowledge of God "unto the perfect man." So once you reach the point where you realize that God has given you the personal responsibility of "fatherhood" for His heritage, then He will begin to say, "I want you *all* to come up higher." That means "we—you all— everybody!"

If you're thinking that will take a miracle, you are right! It is God who will connect you and lock you in with the other members of His Body. It is only through His grace and supernatural intervention and provision that you can begin to understand the "corporateness" of His plan and destiny for the Church.

What You Do Matters to Us All

The children of Israel received a dramatic lesson about their "corporateness" right after they saw the walls of Jericho come falling down during their worship march in the land of Canaan. Confident after such a miraculous victory, Joshua sent a much smaller force to take a tiny city called Ai, but he didn't know that *one man* had dared to ignore God's specific command not to "touch the unclean thing" (see Josh. 7:1-26).

A man named Achan had secretly taken gold and silver from the spoils of Jericho and hid it away. As a result, the army of Israel was totally defeated by tiny Ai, and the entire nation was embarrassed because of *one man's* sin!

God judged all Israel over Achan's private sin. He also judged the church at Corinth because one man in the church was allowed to continue unchallenged in his deviant sexual sin, although it was evidently common knowledge among the members of the church. Paul said in the middle of His judgment, "a little leaven, leavens the whole lump" (1 Cor. 5:1-6).

In the "perfect man" stage, you begin to understand that "what you do affects me, and what I do affects you." The Holy Spirit singled out Ananias and Sapphira for judgment because of their secret sin. He specifically separated them from the church at Jerusalem, possibly because the rest of the church was walking in such unity and obedience to the Lord.

We will come to the knowledge of the "perfect man" when we understand that we are connected and that we need each other. As you begin to understand your "corporateness" as a part of God's Body and break into the level of the "perfect man," your eyes will be opened. When you hear someone say, "I don't want folk in my business," you will know that the person speaking is still operating on a lower level. Ananias and Sapphira's "private business" became everybody's business because the Holy Spirit refused to allow it to bring judgment on the whole body of believers who were being obedient to Him.

The "perfect man" stage is marked by a new understanding: "God not only wants to mature 'me' as an individual, but He wants to make 'us' a perfect man, corporately." You can't become perfect by yourself. In the "perfect man" stage, the Holy Spirit characteristically triggers a "press" or a longing in the people to draw together to fulfill their *corporate destiny*.

A Plural Understanding

You can identify people who are moving from fatherhood to "a perfect man" by their new language of "we" and "us." When you are moving to this new level you won't be content to simply "understand" the broad panorama of God's eternal purposes for the body or to "exercise *your* senses to discern good and evil." Even though you will readily accept personal responsibility for God's true treasure (His children) as a "Father," as a "perfect man," you will also begin to talk almost exclusively in corporate terms of "we" and "us." Even your prayers will change.

You will no longer be satisfied to simply pray for your own needs and issues or for those of other individuals alone. More and more you will also be led by the Spirit to pray for the needs and direction of the corporate body. Your prayers will become intercession as you pray the will of God for your entire church family: "Dear God, bring the church into all that You have prophesied for her to be. Bring *us* unto all that you have prophesied for *us* to be!" Corporate growth and progress into the "perfect man" will only come as we begin to *move together* to press into the things of God.

Once you rise to the "perfect man" level, all your conversation and thoughts will concern "us," not just "me and mine." You're not so concerned with getting the deepest revelation, the latest teaching, or simply "getting fed." You will no longer rush to get "hands laid on you" or to receive a prophecy (although these things are New Testament realities). Now you will be more concerned about "us." You want "us all" to hear from God and be blessed. You will want "us all" to be healed. You won't be satisfied until you see everyone whole, everyone receiving a *rhema* from God, and everyone walking in their divine destiny.

Move on to Perfection

The eleventh chapter of Hebrews contains the great "hall of fame of faith," honoring the people who were looking for a city whose founder and builder was God. The Lord declared these people had obtained their individual victories and revelations. They had even embraced a good report based on the partial revelation that they had centuries before the birth of Christ. Yet God also said *they could not be made perfect* and receive the promise until we came in!

And these all, having obtained a good report through faith, received not the promise: God having provided some better thing for us, that they without us should not be made perfect (Hebrews 11:39-40).

Now the promise has been given. It is obtainable because God is now saying "I am going to turn and bring forth those that want to move on to perfection."

*Therefore leaving the principles of the doctrine of Christ, **let us go on unto perfection**; not laying again the foundation of repentance from dead works, and of faith toward God, of the doctrine of baptisms, and of laying on of hands, and of resurrection of the dead, and of eternal judgment. And this will we do, if God permit* (Hebrews 6:1-3).

You have to go beyond the foundational doctrines of the faith to move on to perfection. God is opening a door, and it is time to go through. The door of Noah's ark was only open for a limited period of time. Noah loaded the animals, the supplies, and his family members into the ark. Then God shut the door, locking out everyone and everything else.

The door to the outer court of the tabernacle in the Old Testament was only open to the public for a specified time. Then then the door was shut. The same was true for priestly ministry to the Lord. There was a time for the priests to come in, then the door was shut. There's also a time for salvation, and then the door will be shut.

I believe that God has given us as the Church an open door to perfection. He is saying, "You can come in, but there is a window of time to enter and to leave." Those who are moving on in the levels of God's glory understand that when God swings open a door, that is the time to go in and sup with Him. We must be sensitive to the times and seasons of the Lord. When there is an open door for us to rise up into a new level of corporate perfection, that is the time we need to behold His face and follow His lead.

"Till we *all* come in the unity of the faith, and of the knowledge of the Son of God, unto a *perfect man*, unto the measure of the stature of the fulness of Christ" (Eph. 4:13). The "perfect man" is concerned with bringing *everyone* into "the measure of the stature of the fulness of Christ." You may say, "That will never happen," but God says differently. Perfection equal to the fullness of Christ Jesus is the goal *God set* for us. I have never seen God set a goal and declare something was going to be less! It does not happen. God sees this goal as already accomplished.

> *Behold, what manner of love the Father hath bestowed upon us, that we should be called the sons of God: therefore the world knoweth us not, because it knew Him not. Beloved, now are we the sons of God, and it doeth not yet appear what we shall be...* (1 John 3:1-2).

John the apostle was aware that a lot of changing was going on. He said, "We are the sons of God, but it doesn't appear what we shall be. This is what we are, and this is what we shall be." Since we are changing, we shouldn't get frustrated about what we "are." We need to keep on reaching and pressing into what we shall be.

The Glorified Man

Lastly, the eighth chapter of Romans talks about the "Glorified Man." This is the glorious Church God will present to Himself, the purified Bride without spot or wrinkle. God sees all this right now. Because He is not bound by time or distance, He sees you perfected and glorified this very moment! He already sees you as a "father" in the faith—at this very moment. You too will adopt this timeless perspective as you move further into God. Less and less will you complain about "what you see" of the beggarly elements of the temporal world. Everything depends on your point of perspective (either you are looking at situations from above or beneath).

If you closely examine the inside of a house at the floor level, you will probably see a lot of dirt, dust, and debris. But if you step outside and look down on the house from above, you'll probably see a beautiful house with nice bushes, and yard. Your perspective depends on your vantage point. That's why I don't get frustrated with folks who don't know how to control their tongue. I know that when they grow in the Lord a little more, they will bring their tongue under subjection as a part of their increasing maturity.

I don't care how many times you shout "Hallelujah" in a service. I'm not impressed or depressed by the outward stress of your intense intercession, nor by how many flowery prophecies you give or receive; if you can't control your tongue, I know you have reached neither the "perfect man" or "Glorious Man" stages yet. If what comes out of your mouth does not speak of the eternal purposes of God, bring us into corporate unity, and or express God's mind, plan, and purposes, then you have not reached the highest levels of maturity. God is inviting all of us together to "come hither...."

Our Glorification Is Predestined

Each stage of development is proper and worthy of acceptance *in its time*. The "babe" stage is not a stage of condemnation because we *all* must pass through this stage. The "child" stage is not a stage of condemnation either. We all must experience childhood in the Kingdom. The same is true of the "young man" and "father" stages, and even the "perfect man" and "Glorified Man" stages.

For whom He did foreknow, He also did predestinate to be conformed to the image of His Son [that is our destiny], *that He might be the firstborn among many brethren. Moreover whom He did predestinate, them He also called: and whom He called, them He also justified: and whom He justified, them He also glorified* (Romans 8:29-30).

God *predestined* us (past tense)! He *called* us (past tense). He *justified* us (past tense), and He *glorified* us (past tense)!

This means that God *already* sees you glorified! He sees you walking in fullness, being all that He has called you to be. In practical terms, the only way you can really prophesy over someone properly is to "see" what God wants to do in that person's life and call him or her forth into that thing. That is what impartation and "activation" is all about. We are to "activate" and bring people into what God has already ordained for them.

John said, "...*we* shall be like Him, for we [corporately] shall see Him as He is" (1 Jn. 3:2). The glorified Body comes when the many members of the corporate Body behold Him and see Him as He is. When we are able to see Him as He is revealed in one another, we are changed. When we are able to see Him revealed as He is in the corporate Body of the Church and as He is in His glorious appearing, then we are changed into that same image and glory.

**To the extent that you behold Him, and
no further, is the extent you will change.**

We are changed into the image of that which we behold. If I can behold Him in the corporate Body of the saints, then I will be changed from glory to glory into that same image and glory. One day He will crack open the sky because He will see us beholding Him in one another. When He looks into the Church, He will behold Himself in us and say, "This is My Bride, My glorious one. I see that she is dressed and ready for My arrival."

For this we say unto you by the word of the Lord, that we which are alive and remain unto the coming of the Lord shall not prevent them which are asleep. For the Lord Himself shall descend from heaven with a shout, with the voice of the archangel, and with the trump of God: and the dead in Christ shall rise first: Then we which are alive and remain shall be caught up together with them in the clouds, to meet the Lord in the air: and so shall we ever be with the Lord (1 Thessalonians 4:15-17).

John the apostle declared, "And I John saw the holy city, new Jerusalem, coming down from God out of heaven, prepared *as a bride* adorned for her husband" (Rev. 21:2). The Bible says the Lord will appear and we will be caught up together. This glorified state is the last corporate thing God will do when He sweeps us all up with a violent motion of change. We will put on immortality, and those who preceded us in death will be brought up and changed first. Then we will be changed in a moment, in a twinkling of an eye, as we are caught up together with Him in the air (1 Cor. 15:52).

A Greater Level of Maturity Waits for You

How do we reach these higher levels of maturity? What are the "processes" or steps we should take? The New

Testament reveals six steps of maturity: babe, child, young man, father, perfect man, and Glorified Man. For each of these major "steps" of maturity, there are at least six more "little steps" to take us higher in our walk with God. The most important thing to remember is that God Himself directs and empowers our growth. Scripture says, "For it is God which worketh in you both to will and to do of His good pleasure" (Phil. 2:13). God says, "Let Me bring you into this next level." He doesn't permit us to take some quantum leap and bypass intermediate steps. He takes us into each level, step by step, through a walk of faith.

The Lord wants us to "*walk* in the Spirit," not *jump* in the Spirit. He wants us to "walk in love," not jump or fall in love. He wants us to "walk in faith," not "take a leap" of faith. We try to run and leap when God is trying to get us to walk! Consider this well-known passage in Isaiah 40: "But they that wait upon the Lord shall renew their strength; they shall mount up with wings as eagles..." (Is. 40:31). Look at the last part of the verse: "They shall run, and not be weary; and they shall walk, and not faint" (Is. 40:31b).

God has been trying to get us to walk for a long time. It is children who typically try to run and jump their way through life. Seasoned and more mature individuals cover the distance through a measured, persistent walking pace. No matter how many shortcuts and fast tracks we try to find, God will have His way as He *walks* us up into new levels of maturity. John gave us a glimpse of God's methodology in his first Epistle:

That which was from the beginning, which we have heard, which we have seen with our eyes, which we have looked upon, and our hands have handled, of the

Word of life; (for the life was manifested, and we have seen it, and bear witness, and shew unto you that eternal life, which was with the Father, and was manifested unto us;) that which we have seen and heard declare we unto you, that ye also may have fellowship with us: and truly our fellowship is with the Father, and with His Son Jesus Christ. And these things write we unto you, that your joy may be full (1 John 1:1-4).

John said, "I saw something, I heard something, I handled something, the Word of life." John longed for us to move into higher levels of revelation. All he could declare was, "That which we have heard; that which our eyes have seen; that which we have looked upon; and that which we have handled, the Word of life."

The first thing you need before you can move into a new level is a revelation that there is a new level awaiting you. You cannot move into what you have not seen, heard, handled, and embraced yourself. This is why Paul wrote, "Work out your own salvation..." (Phil. 2:12b).

Chapter 3

The Desire of God

It is one thing to hear someone stand up and talk about levels of maturity, intercession, prayer, and prophecy; but it is an entirely different thing to experience these things for yourself. No matter how much you read about levels of maturity in this book, the reality of true growth in Christ will only come when you have "handled it, heard it, and seen it" for yourself.

A new revelation of the growth process comes each time you become aware that "where you are" is not all that God wants to do in and through you. Growth is a two-part process. It involves the things that happen to and within you, and it involves the things you are to do and become to others. Although you should never minimize the importance of the fact that you have been "born again," you need to realize that this supernatural experience was only the door—it is up to you to walk through and "enter" into God's purposes for your life.

Press On

Jesus said, "Verily, verily, I say unto thee, Except a man be born of water and of the Spirit, he cannot enter into the kingdom of God" (Jn. 3:5). In Luke 16:16, He said, "The law and the prophets were until John: since that time the kingdom of God is preached, *every man presseth into it.*"

Awareness of new levels may come by preaching, teaching, or proclaiming that "there is more in God than you have right now!" God will sometimes speak to you Spirit to spirit. Sometimes He will speak to you through prophecy. He often speaks through His Word, and there will be times when He will simply plant a burning desire inside of you as you worship and delight yourself in Him. He drops these desires in your heart to let you know that it is time to move on from where you are. It is time to step out of your comfort zone, away from what has become "religious" and lifeless. When we fail to grow and move on, we develop and cherish "a form of godliness, but deny the power thereof" (2 Tim. 3:5). Once the freshness is gone, the anointing is missing, and the keenness is dulled, God will sovereignly drop desire in your heart and say, "There's more of Me than this."

Jesus' statement in the Gospel of John that every man "presses into" the Kingdom is a clear indication that no one will ever reach new levels of spiritual maturity by merely "tiptoeing through the tulips." There has to be a "pressing in" to new levels. If there is not "pressing," then there will be no "progressing" to new levels!

In Luke 22, we see Jesus walking the earth as a priest unto God, as a prophet in the earth, and as a teacher among men—preaching and teaching the Word of God. By the end the chapter, we see Jesus moving on to a new level. He was getting ready to break into His new position as the manifested Lamb of God.

And He came out, and went, as He was wont, to the mount of Olives; and His disciples also followed Him. And when He was at the place, He said unto them, Pray that ye enter not into temptation. And He was withdrawn from them about a stone's cast, and kneeled down, and prayed, Saying, Father, if Thou be willing, remove this cup from Me: nevertheless not My will, but Thine, be done. And there appeared an angel unto Him from heaven, strengthening Him. And being in an agony He prayed more earnestly: and His sweat was as it were great drops of blood falling down to the ground. And when He rose up from prayer, and was come to His disciples, He found them sleeping for sorrow, and said unto them, Why sleep ye? rise and pray, lest ye enter into temptation (Luke 22:39-46).

When John the Baptist saw Jesus years before, at the beginning of His ministry, he said, "Behold, the Lamb of God" (see Jn. 1:29,36). That was not the manifested time for Jesus to become the Lamb of God, but three and a half years passed. The time came for Him to manifest Himself as the Lamb and to do a priestly work at the same time.

When Jesus prayed in the garden, He was "getting into the press." The Bible tells us He was in agony, or *agonitzomore* in the Greek. That word means "to strive, to labor, to fight, and to contend." There is no way to break into any higher level without agony, without fighting, without contending for that particular level. Why? It is because our adversary, the devil, bitterly resists you at every level.

An Uphill Battle

Every level in God is "up." We go from glory to glory, from faith to faith, and from grace to grace. We're always moving up in God, while the accuser of the brethren is continually being cast down under our feet! Our enemy, called the prince of the power of the air, encamps at the higher levels of our world (Eph. 2:2). The only way to take that ground is to put the devil under our feet and press into the new level to which God is calling us.

That is why Paul told Timothy, "Fight the good fight of faith, lay hold on eternal life" (1 Tim. 6:12a). Someone may object, "But don't you just have to say, 'Jesus, I'm sorry for my sins' and 'You're Lord of my life' to receive eternal life?" No, Jesus says you have to *press into it*! Salvation is a free gift, but maturity is a hard-won possession, the fruit of obedience and perseverance in the face of obstacles.

Strive to enter in at the strait gate: for many, I say unto you, will seek to enter in, and shall not be able. When once the master of the house is risen up, and hath shut to the door, and ye begin to stand without, and to knock at the door, saying, Lord, Lord, open unto us; and he shall answer and say unto you, I know you not whence ye are (Luke 13:24-25).

When God opens a door in your life for you to break into a new level, that is the time you must strive. It is interesting that the Greek word for "strive" is the same word used in Luke 22 to describe Jesus' agonizing in the garden. Growth only comes through struggle and perseverance to fulfill God's will.

Many people begin to strive and press into the deeper things of the Christian walk only to draw back when they run into strong resistance. When you withdraw, agony stops. Unfortunately, God's work in your life will probably stop too! The Book of Hebrews says, "Now the just shall live by faith: but if any man draw back, My soul shall have no pleasure in him. But we are not of them who draw back unto perdition; but of them that believe to the saving of the soul" (see Heb. 10:38-39).

You can be one of those who draw back. You can stop going to church because of the agony, and the resistance and agony will definitely stop. Things will seem to go along relatively well again until you once again begin to push into a new level of maturity. Then you may overhear someone talking about you. There might be an assault on your character or even fierce resistance from your family members.

One time when I was pressing into a higher level in my walk with Jesus I began to hear people saying evil and venomous things about me without cause. I said, "God, they're talking about me." The Lord replied, "All they're doing is keeping the woe off of you." This made me pause, so I asked, "Keeping the woe off of me?" And He said, "Yes, remember My words: 'Woe unto you, when all men shall speak well of you!' " (Lk. 6:26a). The Lord explained, "There is a woe when everyone speaks well of you. That means you are doing nothing to offend them or expose their own failure to grow. Keep on coming, let them talk, and break into this higher level." Now whenever folks talk about me, I just say, "Thank you."

Moving Up Together

When the corporate body of a local church moves together into a new level, everyone in that body—no matter what level they are on personally—will feel the pressure. It doesn't matter whether you are a babe, a child, a father, or are moving on into the perfect man. When God calls a local body of believers up to another level, *everybody* feels the pressure. Some will withdraw, saying, "You all go ahead and break into that level. Once you have broken through, you can let me know."

Why does the enemy resist you so much? He knows that when you take that new level, you will also take dominion over every enemy that was trying to block your entrance to that level and place them under your feet! The Lord will remain in Heaven until "the times of restitution of all things" (Acts 3:21). When all things have been subdued and put under our feet, then the last enemy to be subdued will be death. (1 Cor. 15:26) Then Christ will be ready to come and receive His Church unto Himself. There is a certain "striving agony" that we must go through to "enter into" the deeper things of the Kingdom.

Paul declared, "Yea, so have I strived to preach the gospel, not where Christ was named, lest I should build upon another man's foundation" (Rom. 15:20). Paul struggled to preach the gospel where it had never been preached before, and his struggle to obey God against all odds stirred up stiff resistance everywhere he went! The Book of Acts is an open demonstration of the Kingdom of God in growth pains. What did Paul ask the church at Rome to do?

And I am sure that, when I come unto you, I shall come in the fulness of the blessing of the gospel of Christ. Now I beseech you, brethren, for the Lord Jesus Christ's sake, and for the love of the Spirit, that ye strive together with me in your prayers to God for me; that I may be delivered from them that do not believe in Judaea; and that my service which I have for Jerusalem may be accepted of the saints (Romans 15:29-30).

Paul was saying, "I'm sure that when I come to you, I'm coming in fullness because *I'm pressing in*; I'm taking new levels; and I'm coming into the measure of the stature of the fullness of Christ. I'm coming for you all." He was coming as a "perfect man," one who has come into the measure of the stature of the fullness of Christ.

In verse 30, Paul was saying, "I'm praying that you would *strive* for me." The original Greek word here is not *agonitzome*, but the word *sunagonitzome*, which means "a striving corporately of a people for a purpose." That's what corporate intercession is; it's a striving *together* for a specific purpose. Generally in a prayer meeting, everyone brings individual requests and then the participants all go off to pray over their individual requests. Intercessory prayer, on the other hand, involves travail and the birthing of a thing. Corporate intercession should be focused on one thing at one time. That is what the apostle Paul was asking of the Roman believers: "I want you to focus in on one thing. I want you to *strive together with me* in prayer for the sake of the gospel."

Laboring for One Another

I believe that progression at every level involves a certain striving, laboring, and travail. When you are a "babe" in Christ, most of the travail is done by the person who lead you to the Lord. He or she begins to labor, birth, and travail until

"Christ be formed in you" (see Gal. 4:19). They make it their responsibility to help bring you to the next level.

The same thing happens when you reach the level of "child" in the Body of Christ. Someone else bears the responsibility of praying, laboring, and travailing for you, that you "...be strengthened with might by His Spirit in the inner man; that Christ may dwell in your hearts by faith" (Eph. 3:16-17a). At the young man stage, you begin to understand that there are some demonic forces on this level, and you begin to labor, travail, and fight alongside your mentors and instructors as a co-laborer in Christ.

Finally you will come to a point where God will ask you to move on into the "fathers" level. We don't have many believers at the "father" level today, and we need their sense of "corporateness" and their ability to help the whole body begin to sense its corporate destiny. At this level; it is no so much us "fighting into" this level, but rather it is a "pushing prayer" that begins to push on that level en masse, or as a whole.

The enemy has set entrapments and entrenchments of demons to keep people out of that level. Again, entrance only comes with a certain definite laboring and birthing. Paul was saying, "For me to get into these levels I need you all to labor with me in prayer. I need to be more intense. I need to be more focused. I need your united help to penetrate it."

When you labor together with other believers in a particular area or level, you begin to "poke holes in the floor" of that level. Have you ever seen termites go to work on wood? Termites are tiny insects, and when you put these little creatures beside a big beam in the roof or basement of a house, they don't look like they could do much damage.

However, once you get several hundred termites working on a beam of wood, they will start to tunnel in and furrow holes throughout that wood. They start out with just one little hole, but before they are finished (in about 30 days), that thing will collapse if you dare to lean on it. That is a picture of what God wants us to do through intercession and persistent "pressing in." He is saying, "Begin to strive, agonize, and labor. Begin to poke holes in the places that are strongholds of resistance to My will and purposes."

The Road to Corporate Growth

You may feel like giving up when you try to progress to a certain level, and you reach so high only to stall or even fall back at times. Sometimes your praise life may be like that. God will lead you to break into a new level of praise, but you feel like crying! You will ask, "What is wrong with me? Something seems to be blocking my way!" The answer is found in your local body. You need to get some people laboring together with you so you can begin to poke holes in that barrier! All at once, you will break through that thing. Once you break through it, a vacuum will be created. To your amazement, everyone who was laboring with you in prayer will become "sucked up" into that level with you! God will bring everybody up into that next level together because they followed His plan for joint labor in the Spirit.

This is the way spiritual warfare and corporate growth should look: When you are faced with a big black wall separating you from the next level, you begin to poke holes in that barrier through prayer, agonizing, and travail. Then as a unified body of Christ, you will say, to those with whom you labor, "It's time to take it, fellows. It is time for us all to just run through that thing. When you look behind after breaking through to the next level, you should be able to see a "body-sized hole," or silhouette, where you all rushed the barrier together and broke through that thing.

Sanctify Your Current Level

On every level you enter you will find a lot of "dirt and debris." That is why one of the things God has you do each time you enter a new level is to cleanse and sanctify it. When God says, "Come on upstairs," you may be tempted to look at all the "dirt" on that level and think, *I thought the folks up here were spiritual.* But God asks, "Can you see your brother's defilement, wash his feet, and keep on working with him?" That is a lesson that must be learned. Can you wash your brother's feet even while he is in his defilement and his pride? When you see him naked and drunk, will you cover him instead of broadcasting his nakedness?

When everybody else is sitting around a table talking about where they're going to be in the Kingdom, can you pick up a bowel and towel and wash their feet? When they've denied you, betrayed you, and turned their backs on you, can you say as Jesus said to Peter, "Do you love Me? Feed My sheep" (see Jn. 21:16-17). Jesus was saying, "Look Peter, you have been thinking about all the great things that have been done, and the great preaching that you would do. But all the time, it's been about love. All I want to know is if you love Me. You didn't have to stand up and say, 'I'll drink of that cup with You. I'll go to the cross with You.' All I want to know is, 'Do you love Me?' "

When one level is cleansed, God says, "Come on upstairs." When you've worked from the "basement" up to the "main level," guess what? There's no automatic cleansing system at that level either. You still have to go through each bedroom, bathroom, and hallway to cleanse away the debris and dirt.

What happens then? God will swing open an attic door! When most folks get to the attic, they become tired and say, "I'm never going to use the attic anyway. It's hot up there, and loads of dirt have built up in the corners. (The higher you go, the thicker the dirt will be, for fewer people reach those levels because of what they see there.) Some people get so discouraged because of the dirt and defilement they see in the brethren on this level that they never want to enter it. The way is blocked by entrenched principalities and dirt, but God has ordained, equipped, and called us to clean that level.

God says, "Yes, there's dirt up here, but I will break you into it if you will cleanse that level once you enter it." This is where things like backbiting, gossip, and malice come in. Some people break through to a new level, without really understanding that they are not there to criticize and talk about the "dirt" they see in other people on that level—they are to go to work lifting up, cleansing, and covering their brethren while also examining their own lives.

When you speak evil and criticize other believers, you are only "adding more dirt to the dirt." That means the next person who comes along will have two big messes to clean up instead of one. In each level of maturity, God expects us to clean up the messes we see and to always wash our brothers' feet and cover their faults. Once the level is cleansed through obedience, we should then say, "Now let's work together, brethren. Let's begin to poke holes in the next barrier so we can enter that next level." Once you understand this, you will understand why God lets you see both His glory and man's defilement at the same time (that is what He sees in you!). God is saying, "Pursue the glory; cleanse the defilement!"

Life Through Death

We break into each new level of maturity with agony. I can assure you that when you get involved in that agony, there will be others who have managed even worse situations. The Book of Hebrews says, "Ye have not yet resisted unto blood, striving against sin" (Heb. 12:4).

In other words, none of us experienced the agony that Jesus endured in the garden of Gethsemane as He felt all the pressures of the flesh, the world, the devil, and the overt plans of men pressing down on Him. He prayed with such great intensity that He couldn't even find someone to join in agreement with Him. The intercession was intense because the agony was so intense.

Now that Jesus has paid the price, our Father has placed us in His Body, the Church. Now we can say, like Paul, "Labor together with me, and strive together with me in prayer." Let's pray more earnestly so we can break into these various levels in God.

Each level of maturity also contains a "level of death" that must be passed through. In a sense, each of these levels is actually a death and resurrection to the new level—representing a new life on another plane! There can be no life until there's been a death. First, there is an entrance into resurrection on one level or life. Then when you reach the end of it and you are just ready to break through to the next level, your agony will become so intense that you experience a "death." Through that death, you break into new life at another level.

But if our gospel be hid, it is hid to them that are lost: In whom the god of this world hath blinded the minds of them which believe not, lest the light of the glorious gospel of Christ, who is the image of God, should shine unto them (2 Corinthians 4:3-4).

The enemy is at work blinding those to whom we want to bring the good news. Every time you want to bring people out of the level of sin unto the level of the new birth, the enemy goes to work and brings resistance. That's why there must be intercession and breakthrough before there is new life.

The Birth Process

Paul wrote in Galatians 4:19, "My little children, of whom I travail in birth again until Christ be formed in you." He had to labor for the Galatians the first time to bring them to salvation, but then he said, "I have to labor again (as in childbirth) so that Christ be formed in you." No one moves up, no one is birthed into the Kingdom, without a certain degree of agony and co-laboring in prayer. This is because the enemy wants to blind the minds of those to whom you are sent to lead to new levels.

For we preach not ourselves, but Christ Jesus the Lord; and ourselves your servants for Jesus' sake. For God, who commanded the light to shine out of darkness, hath shined in our hearts, to give the light of the knowledge of the glory of God in the face of Jesus Christ. But we have this treasure in earthen vessels, that the excellency of the power may be of God, and not of us (2 Corinthians 4:5-7).

God has commanded that light should shine in darkness. Each level you enter may seem dark, and it may seem like there can be no passage through it. Yet God says, "I have commanded that My light shine in there." Either we will become His light-bearers in that level, or somebody else will become the light. The truth is that you have the light inside of you that can light up and bring revelation to that level. God has "shined in our hearts, to give the light of the knowledge of the glory of God in the faith of Jesus Christ. But we have this treasure in earthen vessels, that the excellency of the power may be of God, and not of us" (2 Cor. 4:6b-7).

Never Forsaken

Paul followed these statements with a graphic description of the agony and struggle he faced as an apostle of God:

We are troubled on every side, yet not distressed; we are perplexed, but not in despair; persecuted, but not forsaken; cast down, but not destroyed; always bearing about in the body the dying of the Lord Jesus, that the life also of Jesus might be made manifest in our body (2 Corinthians 4:8-10).

We have to keep in mind where God is taking us and understand that the agony and the resistance we are experiencing is part of an important fight for a cause. The enemy and circumstances may try to stop us, but we must fight the fight and cleanse that level as we reach for the glory of God. We may be perplexed, but we will not despair. Sometimes we say, "Did God really say this? Was the prophecy true? Did I really hear God on this, or is this just me?"

We may be persecuted, but we will never be forsaken (we have God's Word on it). We may feel cast down, but we will not be destroyed even if the enemy assaults us on that level. From time to time, we may have to stop along the way and step back to the last level we were on. There we can pick ourselves up and repair the shield of faith, put on the breastplate again, straighten up our helmet of salvation, sharpen our sword, gird our loins about with truth, put on the shoes of the preparation of the gospel once again. Then we can charge right back to that level and resist steadfastly, knowing that we have done all to stand. Then we will simply stand against the enemy (see Eph. 6:10-18).

Paul said, "[We are] always bearing about in the body the dying of the Lord Jesus, that the life also of Jesus might be made manifest in our body" (2 Cor. 4:10). Everyone who understands these levels knows that if the life of God is going to be manifested, we must bear in our bodies the dying of the Lord Jesus Christ.

I often hear people quote the apostle Paul and say, "I want to know Him [Jesus Christ] in the power of His resurrection" (see Phil. 3:10a). However, I have read the rest of the verse and found out that I also need to "know Him" in the "fellowship of His suffering" and be made "conformable unto His death." We may not like it, but there is no resurrection without suffering and death!

Paul wrote, "For we which live are alway delivered unto death for Jesus' sake, that the life also of Jesus might be made manifest in our mortal flesh" (2 Cor. 4:11). Where does this take place? In Heaven? No, it takes place right here in our mortal flesh. God wants to make the life of Jesus manifest (or "publicly shine") through you. How does it come forth? It is revealed through a certain resistance, a holy agony, and certain godly striving and fighting for the purposes of God. Yet it is through this struggle that God's life and light breaks forth out of you.

Paul said, "So then death worketh in us, but life in you" (2 Cor. 4:12). Unless there's a death that works in me, there can be no life in anyone else that I touch. Jesus said, "...Except a corn of wheat fall into the ground and die, it abideth alone: but if it die, it will bringeth forth much fruit" (Jn. 12:24). Any living thing that wants to break into the level of fruitfulness must first die in one way or another.

We having the same spirit of faith, according as it is written, I believed, and therefore have I spoken; we also believe, and therefore speak; knowing that He which raised up the Lord Jesus shall raise up us also by Jesus, and shall present us with you. For all things are for your sakes (2 Corinthians 4:13-15a).

Just as God the Father raised Jesus from death to a new level, He will also raise you up to a new level each time you die to something according to His will. Godly people are praying, interceding, pushing, and laboring together with you; and God Himself is beckoning you with His mighty hand, saying, "Come on up, son. Come up here, daughter."

Not Called Alone

The time to climb is when you know you have made that connection, when God has your hand and there is someone behind you pushing you upward on their shoulders. You know what I'm talking about if you have ever tried to climb a tree. Sometimes it takes the assistance of someone in the tree above you and someone on the ground below. Sometimes all you need is a little boost—that is the job of intercessors and prayer warriors. They give you and me a "boost."

God will raise you up. You will come forth. That's why I'm not discouraged about the condition of the Church. I know what God has said. I'm going forward and pressing towards the mark. God has assured me that if I press into everything He has called me to, then He will gather people around me who will press into it with me.

God is faithful to raise up crazy, radical, and seemingly foolish people who will say, "It's good on this level, brother, but we know there's more!" Sometimes people will walk by me and say, "There's more." I just reply, "I know." That's all I can say. I can't speak of the defilement I see. I can't speak of the problems I see. I just say, "I know. I acknowledge there's more." And there *is* more to come, but we will have to press into it.

Paul said, "For which cause we faint not..." (2 Cor. 4:16). We *could faint* in the press of battle, but that wasn't Paul's point. He said, *"For which cause...."* Once you see what God wants to bring to pass, you will finally resolve forever in your heart, "I'm not going to quit until I see everything God has promised. Yes, there is resistance, and the enemy wants to bring despair and perplexity, but I am not going to quit. I won't quit until I see us come into everything God promised us!"

You have to have a goal, a direction, a course of action. God has to show you something. Then you can resolve, "I'm not going to stop until I get it." If God humbles you by saying, "You can't get it by yourself on this level," then you need to say, "Brethren, will you strive together with me. Help me get it. Labor together in your prayers and help me press into this thing."

"For which cause we faint not; but though our outward man perish, yet the inward man is renewed day by day" (2 Cor. 4:16). When you get into struggle and agony, God won't wait untill the end of the fight to refresh you. He will bring you a refreshing and a renewing day by day. Each day you can lift your hands and say, "Give me this day my daily bread. Help me to fight the good fight today. Today when I hear your voice, I'll not harden my heart." Enter into His presence and be renewed day by day.

That is why Paul, when referring to the struggles of this life, said, "For our light affliction, which is but for a moment, worketh for us a far more exceeding and eternal weight of glory" (2 Cor. 4:17). How could Paul say this? He explains it in the next verse: "While we look not at the things which are seen, but at the things which are not seen: for the things which are seen are temporal; but the things which are not seen are eternal" (2 Cor. 4:18).

Get Ready for the Life to Come Forth!

Do you have some "not-seen stuff" that you've embraced, subdued, and brought into your bosom? I'm talking about heavenly things you've "seen" only in your spirit. You've tasted of them and desired them. The image has become so real that you want it, and you have said to God, "I'm ready to strive and labor for this. I'm not going to let go until I get it.

"That is what I call a "burning desire." This is what God wants to be in you.

God told the woman in the garden of Eden (a picture of the Church, the Bride of the Last Adam), when she sinned, "I will greatly multiply thy sorrow and thy conception; in sorrow thou shalt bring forth children; and thy desire shall be to thy husband, and he shall rule over thee" (Gen. 3:16b). When God declares it is time to give birth to the godly things He has planted within you, the birth of that thing can be painful. Sometimes, once when we've given birth to a new level, we don't ever want to "get pregnant" again!

Many women tell stories about the time they were about to give birth to a child. Some smile and say, "My husband came up and said, 'I love you,' and all I could say at the time was, 'Don't touch me! I don't ever want to go through this again. Just stay away from me—don't look at me, don't touch me.' " The gestation process and bringing forth new life is hard.

God told Eve in Genesis 3:16, "Thy desire shall be to thy husband." God will come to us one day and say, "You can stay on that level and 'be touchy' if you like. But if you let Me, I'll drop a new desire in your heart. I'm your husband, and I'll drop a new desire in your heart and make you pregnant again." You know the rest of the story. When you find you are pregnant again, you begin to look to the "joy set before you" at the next level and say, "I've got to go there. There is a new life ready to come forth!"

Chapter 4

New Levels of Acceptance

Do you sense that God is calling you to a new level in Him? It is important for you understand what God is going to do when He brings you into that new level. In the Book of Acts, Paul and Barnabas encouraged believers in cities they had previously visited: "Confirming the souls of the disciples, and exhorting them to continue in the faith, that *we must through much tribulation* enter into the kingdom of God" (Acts 14:22). Paul and Barnabas didn't tell these converts they would "go around" tribulation, but *that they would go through* it. When the enemy throws up an obstacle of tribulation, we have to go through it to enter the Kingdom of God.

A Multi-National Body

One of the most powerful things about the Kingdom of God is mentioned by John in Revelation 7:9: "After this I beheld, and, lo, a great multitude, which no man could number...." This multitude was of *every nation, every kindred, every people and every tongue.* The word, *kindred* means "tribe or clan." God is bringing in people from every tribe and every clan. He is also bringing people to Himself out of every tongue, or language and cultural group. Within each of these, there are "people groups," such as children, young people, and adults, poor people and rich people. No one is exempt from God's Kingdom; it includes all kinds of people.

God is redeeming His children out of every nation in the earth. "Every nation" is translated from the Hebrew word *ethnos*. This is also the root of the English word, *ethnic*. There are several major ethnic groups categorized by general skin color: black, white, yellow, red, and brown. The tenth chapter of the Book of Genesis lists 70 distinct nations that descended from Noah's three sons: Shem, Japheth, and Ham. (It is interesting that in Luke 10:1 Jesus dispatched 70 disciples to preach the gospel and declare the Kingdom. The Sanhedrin of Jesus day was also made up of 70 spiritual men who judged Israel.)

When God calls us to new levels, He also calls us to new levels of revelation and to new levels of *acceptance* of one another. If you look at the various people, tongues, ethnic groups, and nations represented in your local church and in the Church worldwide, you'll see various people goups inside of every ethnic group. You'll see rich folks and poor folks, the "haves" and the "have nots" worshiping God side by side. You'll see the incorporated and the unincorporated, the employed and non-employed in every different people group. God is saying, "This is what I am bringing together."

It is obvious that God sees our differences—after all, He created us this way. Yet they don't make a difference to Him, because God doesn't look "after the flesh," but "after the spirit." He looks at the heart, not the skin or outward appearance (aren't you glad?). If we were each able to step out of our outer garment of skin and cosmetic physical features, we would all look the same. God recognizes our differences in personality, nationality, families, kindreds, and tongues, but He is glorified when we disregard these differences to dwell together in unity in His Son.

The panorama John paints in the Book of Revelation of the multi-national community of God seems to prove that God considers our unity in the presence of differences to be a major blessing of His Kingdom. We need to grow and mature to the level where we are able to see that God is not exclusive—He is inclusive. Everyone is welcome in His house, as long as they enter through the blood of the Lamb.

We need to see the Church as God sees it. The Bible reveals a God who looks at the Body of believers and sees representatives from every people group on earth. He says, "That is My Body. These are My people. Each of them has his own unique characteristics and individual differences. Each of My creations brings unique cultural pieces, pleasures, and benefits to My banqueting table. That is good," He says. "That is mankind."

*And one of the elders answered, saying unto me, What are these which are arrayed in white robes? and whence came they? And I said unto him, Sir, thou knowest. And he said to me, These are they which came out of **great tribulation,** and have washed their robes, and made them white in the blood of the Lamb. Therefore are they before the throne of God, and serve Him day and night in His temple: and He that sitteth on the throne shall dwell among them* (Revelation 7:13-15).

This passage echoes the words of Paul who said, "Through much tribulation enter into the kingdom of God" (Acts 14:22b).

I need to step away from the context of this Scripture for a moment to make an important point about relationships in the Church. Tribulation and struggle are "colorblind," just as God's will is colorblind. He has ordained that we advance to perfection *together* as one people—whether we like it or not.

Tribulation and trouble will come every time we press into relationships that cross man-made racial barriers, and ethnic and cultural lines. If we are going to press together into the levels of the perfect man and the glorified man, then we will have to press through tribulation! God is going to break everything that has divided us from one another. Through the Body of Christ in the earth, He's going to put His foot on it and put down every barrier. God is out to do such a thorough inner work in us that when we look at our brothers and sisters all we will see is Christ.

God Looks on the Heart

God is bringing us to the place Jesus described to sceptical and critical Pharisees: "Ye judge after the flesh; I judge no man" (Jn. 8:15). He sees us no longer measuring a man's stature by his social, political, or economic position, nor by the color of his skin. We will measure one another solely by the character of Christ that exudes and comes from the heart. God has always done this, and He is doing it now.

John said the people in the heavenly vision "washed their robes and made them white in the blood of the Lamb" (Rev. 7:14). Washing with water takes care of the exterior things.

But John said "[they] made them white in the blood of the Lamb." The color white speaks of purity. These believers had allowed the cleansing blood of Christ to "dig down" past the surface of the flesh, removing every stain and source of defilement. John saw them standing righteous and perfect in the presence of God.

God has never been satisfied with mere outward appearances. He always goes deeper than "skin deep." God goes straight for the heart. John the Baptist came first, prophesying that the Kingdom of God was at hand (Mt. 3:2). Then Jesus officially opened His public ministry by reading Isaiah's prophecy about the supernatural *demonstration* and *proclamation* of the Kingdom. When He closed the scroll of the prophet, He calmly announced to people in the synogogue, "This day is this scripture *fulfilled* in your ears" (Lk. 4:21b).

For three and a half years, Jesus healed the sick, cast out devils, and preached the good news of the Kingdom. He also taught His disciples about true righteousness of the heart through His own life and ministry. Jesus taught disciple and student alike to question the deepest motives of their heart. Sacrifices could no longer purify the soul. Outward rites of sanctification only deal with the flesh, but Christ came to sanctify the soul itself.

Peter's Prejudice Problem

Jesus wants to bring us all past the "Peter problem." Do you remember Peter's struggle with religious and racial prejudice? This lead apostle in the Church was a Jewish believer who had received a direct revelation that salvation through Christ was for *all men*—regardless of race or national heritage. Yet Peter became so content to "rejoice in Jerusalem" that he wouldn't take the good news to the lost. He wanted to bask in the revival fires of Jerusalem while God was saying, "Get out to the world." (Does this sound familiar?)

Peter only made it out to the *Jewish* communities in Judea. Somehow, he just couldn't make his way to the lost people in "second-class" Samaria. Then God took stronger measures. He allowed persecution to hit Jerusalem, and everyone in the Church but the apostles were scattered. Philip alone among all the apostles finally went to Samaria to preach the gospel. Acts 8 tells us that Philip sparked a great revival there, and that the apostles in Jerusalem sent Peter and John to join Philip there. Peter and John initially overcame their doubts and layed their hands on the Samarians, who received the baptism of the Holy Spirit. They returned Jerusalem again, and God sent Philip to meet a high ranking Ethiopian eunuch in the wilderness and baptize him in Jesus' name.

When we meet Peter again in Acts 10, he is *still* struggling with the concept of non-Jews being saved and filled with the Holy Spirit. When Cornelius, a devout Italian centurion in Caesariea, prayed for a move of the Spirit, God spoke to Peter in a vision, "Get up there to Caesarea and minister to this Italian—and don't doubt" (see Acts 10:9-23).

God knew Peter had a natural dislike of Italians (or Romans) because they had occupied his nation and kept his people in bondage. God literally put him in a trance and dropped a vision before him of a banquet table with *all kinds* of food. Then God said in the vision, "Rise up, slay and eat" (Acts 10:13). Peter basically said, "Lord, You know I'm Jewish! I don't eat pasta, pizza, and spaghetti. I don't even like garlic." But God said, "Rise up, slay, and eat." Peter replied, "I can't handle this stuff." God actually had to deal with him three times to get him motivated and stimulated to go to Caesarea. It took three visions and a trance to hammer the truth into this guy!

When Peter finally made it to Caesarea and met the family of Cornelius in his home, they said, "Peter, good to see you, what took you so long?" He said, "Of the truth I perceive that God is no respecter of persons" (Acts 10:34b). (Well, I imagine so, after all the visions and trances and sheets coming down out of Heaven, and with God telling him three times to rise up, slay, and eat. I guess he could say that God is no respecter of persons.)

Even after he preached at Caesarea, Peter still had problems. In the Book of Galatians, Paul made it clear that Peter still had problems in Galatia, which unlike Caesarea, was way beyond the borders of Israel and Judea.

But when Peter was come to Antioch, I withstood him to the face, because he was to be blamed. For before that certain came from James, he did eat with the Gentiles: but when they were come, he withdrew and separated himself, fearing them which were of the circumcision (Galatians 2:11-12).

When the religious Jewish brothers from the big city arrived, Peter suddenly withdrew from the Gentiles to fellowship exclusively with the Jews. It became so bad that even Paul's old mentor, Barnabas, got carried away by the foolishness. Paul said, "When I heard about it, I decided to confront Peter face to face, and tell him this is not the way of the Lord."

God-Established Relationships

Not only does God want us to come through the tribulation, He also wants us to have new garments, and a new identity that has been washed, cleansed, and made white through the blood of the Lamb. The Book of Acts declares that God "hath made of one blood all nations of men" (Acts 17:26).

The people in John's vision were before the throne of God, and they served Him night and day (Rev. 7:15). Once you break through this barrier and enter this level, you will be in the abiding presence of the Lord. God cannot commit to an abiding presence right now because we would try to merchandise it and make it exclusive. Yet once He cracks this barrier, God does a work in and through us. We begin to say, "I'm not ashamed to be called your brother." We are able to move through and be in His presence all the time.

We will serve Him night and day, and our service will be acceptable because we'll be in His temple. Our service won't be based on doing, it will be based on relationship. God is saying a lot of things to us on different levels concerning relationship. Some hear Him telling us to press into relationship in the Spirit. To other people, God seems to be moving in certain geographical areas.

I'm amazed at the way God is lifting people from one church and putting them in another for specific purposes. Some people have asked Him, "Why are you doing this?" His answer was, "I want you in a different kind of relationship." These folks usually don't really want to move to a new fellowship, but God tells them, "I know it, but I need you here right now. You need to learn some lessons."

God is motivating us to open our houses and break bread together. Your house is where you live. It is a personal expression or extension of your "self." When a man and woman let you into their house, they let you step into an intimate part their life. God has begun to show us that we don't have to be embarrassed about this outward expression of ourselves.

"Well, all I have is just this little dinky apartment." Well, we each used to have a little dinky apartment, and some of us just had one room. "Well, it's not clean." Clean it up, or invite us in with the dirt. (We've seen dirt before. Come over to our house right now and check out the sink. (That's not a negative statement against my wife—but sometimes we just take a break because we get tired.) If you come over and see dishes in our sink and say, "My gosh!" I'll probably just say, "Jump in there and wash them." We need to learn the truth in the verse that says "There is therefore now no condemnation to them which are in Christ Jesus, who walk not after the flesh, but after the Spirit" (Rom. 8:1).

Invite people over and create space for other people in your life. Don't worry so much about externals. Everyone has seen dirty carpet before, and most people in the industrialized nations have eaten from paper plates before. Most of us have even eaten using mismatched silverware and lived to tell about it! When we invite people into our homes and extend true hospitality, we are giving them a space in our lives. God just looks on and says, "Come on in, come and dine with Me, come and dine." That is the heart of God.

God is calling us into His *abiding* presence, not some temporary relationship marked on a church social calendar. God says, "There's more than this!" Let's connect, let's unite. As we do that, God will begin to speak sovereignly to and through His people.

This kind of life in the very presence of God is a "sure cure" for the loneliness that seems to haunt many church bodies. I once told a friend, "Look, no one reaches out here. No one really gets touched in this church." He said, "LaFayette, if you haven't been touched, then reach out yourself! Just reach out." I became a reaching person. I began to grab folks in the body and say, "I'm not going to let you go." Some of my minister friends have said to me, "Well, we'll see you whenever we see you again." I just had to reply, "Oh, no, we're in a relationship now. We're tough to get rid of. Once we connect with you, we are there for life." Are you "tough to get rid of"? My wife and I are like the poor…you will "always have us with you" (see Mt. 26:11).

A Flow of Life

God is not interested in "surface service," He wants us to serve Him day and night "in the temple." We are His holy temple, built up into Him. We are to serve Him day and night in the temple. The Bible doesn't stop there. Look closely at what God's Word says next:

And He that sitteth on the throne shall dwell among them. They shall hunger no more, neither thirst any more; neither shall the sun light on them, nor any heat. For the Lamb which is in the midst of the throne shall feed them, and shall lead them unto living fountains of waters: and God shall wipe away all tears from their eyes (Revelation 7:15b-17).

Hunger and thirst will cease because there is a "feeding," or continual flow of life and nourishment within your brothers and sisters. A refreshing river of living water springs up out of your bellies, and there is a new word inside you. You will hunger and thirst no more because righteousness is being fulfilled as Jesus promised in Matther 5:6, in the "Sermon on the Mount."

God is beginning to condition and prepare us for a great move of God. How is this going to take place? It is already happening in the heavens. Now God wants to manifest it in the earth.

And when he had opened the seventh seal, there was silence in heaven about the space of half an hour. And I saw the seven angels which stood before God; and to them were given seven trumpets. And another angel came and stood at the altar, having a golden censer; and there was given unto him much incense, that he should offer it with the prayers of all saints upon the golden altar which was before the throne. And the smoke of the incense, which came with the prayers of the saints, ascended up before God out of the angel's hand. And the angel took the censer, and filled it with fire of the altar, and cast it into the earth: and there were voices, and thunderings, and lightnings, and an earthquake (Revelation 8:1-5).

This passage is the only record of a time when Heaven was silent. So if you like a real quiet atmosphere and a real quiet church, you get exactly a half hour of silence when you get into glory. (Basically, no matter where you go after physical death, there will be noise—whether its the noisy uninhibited praise of the saints, or the heartrending and unending screams and agonized groans of the damned.) I think that God provides this space of half an hour to give the religious people a chance to adjust.

God is getting ready to do something brand new in this passage. Consider the angel with the golden sensor who was "given...much incense to offer with prayers of the saints." This was done to break forth a new generation that will be drawn from every nation, every kindred, and every tongue. When the prayers of the saints are offered up, angelic warfare will take place against the entrenched demonic forces trying to prevent the advance of the Church to the glorified level. Yet, this will never happen until we come to new levels of acceptance and unconditional love, one for another.

Chapter 5

Breaking Through the Shaking

The problem with any discussion or teaching about "spiritual maturity" is that we tend to make it too theoretical, and forget the realities of life. The truth is that most of the people who obey God and pioneer a new path by cracking through into the level where they break racial bondages and separation are eventually killed.

Throughout recorded history, the enemy has corrupted men and sent them to assassinate those who have tried to break through this barrier into the level of brotherly love. None of this is a "surprise" to God. The messenger angels in Revelation 7 are God's preordained answer to the evil designs of the enemy. God always has a plan to bring His purposes to pass.

God is saying, "Not only must there be prayers of the saints, but the power of My messenger angels must be united with the intercession of the saints." I believe that God has reserved certain angels specifically for this moment, and for this hour. We won't be warring by ourselves any more. The angel of God has been dispatched in power with the golden sensor to offer up the prayers of the saints upon the golden altar before His throne. When the smoke and the incense from the prayers of the saints ascend before God out of the angel's hands, he will take the sensor and fill it full of fire from the altar and cast it into the earth. The Bible says John heard and saw "voices, and thunderings, and lightenings, and an earthquake" (Rev. 8:5).

What do earthquakes symbolize and foreshadow in the Bible? Part of the process of "pressing into new levels" is to understand what God wants to do when He shakes the earth.

See that you refuse not Him that speaketh. For if they escaped not who refused him that spake on earth, much more shall not we escape, if we turn from Him that speaketh from heaven: whose voice shook the earth: but now He hath promised, saying, Yet once more I shake not the earth only, but also heaven (Hebrews 12:25-26).

The last days will be marked by more than an earthquake or two. There will also be a shaking in Heaven. I believe that God Himself will speak, and the principalities that have not permitted or have prevented us from breaking into certain levels of unity will be smashed and shaken.

Shaking Up Systems

What is the shaking for? "And this word, Yet once more, signifieth the removing of those things that are shaken, as of things that are made, that those things which cannot be shaken may remain" (Heb. 12:27). We've made up a lot of systems, rules, regulations, and reasons to justify why we can't get it all together. But God says, "I'm going to shake not only the earth, but I'm going to shake the heavens. And I will remove everything that has been made up by man that cannot withstand My shaking."

Whenever earthquakes occur, "faults" also appear in the earth. Faults are movements of large segments of the earth. An earthquake occurs when one level or section of the earth's crust moves up while another level remains in place or moves downward. When the opposing forces move the earth, the energy released is called an earthquake. Scientists measure this energy on a scale of intensity called the Richter scale.

If you will look through the Bible, you will find that every time a new dispensation of God comes to a city or people, it is nearly always preceded by an earthshaking episode. When Christ said from the cross, "It is finished" (Jn. 19:30), the earth shook. Three days later, when Christ came out of the tomb, the earth shook again. When Paul went to Philippi and was thrown into jail for confronting residents who had been given over to soothsaying and devils, the saints began to pray with one voice—and the earth shook.

According to the passage we quoted earlier from Hebrews 12, God is going to shake the earth again, as well as the heavens. Even the demons and principalities that have hindered us from moving into all that God has for us— even these spirit beings are going to shake:

> ...Now He hath promised, saying, Yet once more I shake not the earth only, but also heaven. And this

word, Yet once more, signifieth the removing of those things that are shaken, as of things that are made, that those things which cannot be shaken may remain. Wherefore we receiving a kingdom which cannot be moved, let us have grace, whereby we may serve God acceptably with reverence and godly fear: For our God is a consuming fire (Hebrews 12:26-29).

Rout the Enemy

God is preparing to do an abiding work of eternal weight in glory. God will work together with us on the earth while releasing and joining together the timeless prayers of the saints and the power of His angels in the heavenlies. The angels will wage deadly warfare from above and we will wage war with His Word and presence from beneath. This way the enemy will be "bombed" from above and beneath at the same time! Every time we send up praise and intercession from below, our spiritual actions literally return to assault the enemy.

What happens when an enemy force is assaulted from both the ground and the air (as in Operation Desert Storm)? Any enemy assaulted simultaneously from above and below is doomed. God is causing us to actively focus our prayer and assault. I believe the day has come when God is moving us beyond "complaining about what we see" to prophesying into existence what should be, and prophesying death to everything that should not be! God is saying, "Speak the Word of the Lord. Prophesy to the winds; command them to come. Cause the dry and separated bones in the valley to hear the Word of the Lord." This is the command of God to us at every level of maturity.

The writer of Hebrews says, "Let us have grace, whereby we may serve God acceptably with reverence and godly fear" (Heb. 12:28b). When he says, "Let us have grace..." he is saying, "Let us have that divine enablement, that ability that God gives—not only to sow a desire in our heart, but to cultivate it, water it, bring it forth, and perform the very thing that He sewn in our heart."

The Purifying Fire

God is baptizing His Church with fire. That is why you feel the heat right now. The Bible speaks of more than water baptism and the baptism of the Holy Ghost. There is also a "baptism with fire."

> *...He shall baptize you with the Holy Ghost, and with fire: whose fan is in His hand, and He will throughly purge His floor, and gather His wheat into the garner; but He will burn up the chaff with unquenchable fire* (Matthew 3:11-12).

Wood, hay, and stubble, the fleshly works in our lives, will pass away in the flames of God's baptism of fire. But the holy things, the things we build of gold, silver, and precious stones, will remain. Gold represents the deity of God, silver the redemption of God, and precious stones are the living stones of the people of God. Fire only refines these precious elements, causing them to show forth more brilliance than before. When precious stones, gold, and silver melt down, they present a mirror-like surface or facet. When God looks in our fire-cleansed and illuminated mirror, He sees Himself and says, "That is what I've wanted all along. I have wanted to see Myself in My Church, but there was so much dust and chaff that I had to turn on the heat. The cleansing and the shaking is why you will now receive a Kingdom that *cannot* be shaken."

Something Better Is on the Way

This idea of "receiving the Kingdom" is one of a process, a continuous thing rooted in our growth in Christ. As I pace and pray each morning, saying, "I thank You that we're receiving a Kingdom" the Kingdom comes. The very next morning, I pray again, and it keeps on coming, again and again. Each time, I receive fuller understanding, yet it keeps on coming. I get more divine revelation, yet it keeps on coming. I get more experience, but it keeps on coming. I see increased manifestation of His Kingdom in my life, my ministry, and the local body, yet it keeps on coming!

How long will this continue? It will continue until I am walking in His fullness; until Christ Himself is manifest in all of His glory; until I see Him and behold Him face to face as He is. God is saying to you and I, "I am calling you up to this level. This is where I want you to be and who I want you to be. Don't shrink back and fall short of My best. Keep pressing into My presence."

*But, beloved, we are persuaded **better things** of you, and things that accompany salvation, though we thus speak. For God is not unrighteous to forget your work and labour of love, which ye have shewed toward His name, in that ye have ministered to the saints, and do minister* (Hebrews 6:9-10).

Some people had some things that were good, and others had some things that were acceptable, but God said, "We're persuaded of *better things* for you...."

"Which hope we have as an anchor of the soul, both sure and stedfast, and which entereth into that within the veil" (Heb. 6:19). Why are we spending so much time and space talking about these new levels? I have found that if you don't have a hope for a new level, then you never learn how to focus and believe God for it. We all need to have hope, the "expectation of favorable change." The Word of God tells us that our hope is an anchor for our souls.

Hope reassures us that "what you see is not all that there is to be." When God's Word says, "I'm persuaded of better things than this for you," He is saying, "What you see is not all that there is to be. I have desired even better things for you. I want you to remain faithful, full of assurance, till the end."

And we desire that every one of you do shew the same diligence to the full assurance of hope unto the end: that ye be not slothful, but followers of them who through faith and patience inherit the promises (Hebrews 6:11-12).

What Are You Fighting For?

It takes faith and patience to break into higher levels of maturity and obedience. Sometimes we have the faith, but we get upset when progress just doesn't happen for us "right now." At other times, we seem to have the patience of Job, but we act like we don't even know what we're waiting for. Even if it showed up, we wouldn't know it.

"Well, I'm just waiting."
"What are you waiting for?"
"Oh, I'm just waiting for my change to come."
"What kind of change? What are you waiting on?"

It is fine to "wait" if you know what you are waiting on. However, if you don't know what you're waiting on, then it may come and go and you'll never know it was there. In a way, faith and patience are "twins." Faith is the God-given ability to reach into the Spirit realm to hear a fresh word from God on your situation and to take hold of that thing until it becomes the substance of things hoped for, the proof, or title deed of things not seen (see Heb. 11:1). It is the ability to get into agreement with what God says is going to be so.

Your "war" is not against any person who is trying to get you to do something. You have already said what you will do. You have the "title deed" right there in your hand. You just need to "war" against anything that comes in violation, in assault, or in an adversarial attitude against the thing God has spoken.

When God says, "How long are you willing to fight?" I tell Him, "I'm willing to fight until I win. Give me a word, Lord, and I'll be ready to stand." Why? Because once I get a word from God, I have the title deed! And once I get the title deed, I'm ready to stand. Every time something comes along to challenge my right to God's treasures—whether it be man, woman, demon, principality, power, might, or dominion—I just show them my "title deed." I don't care what they say because I know I have the word of the Lord on the issue. I just say, "I know what God has said. That is the word of the Lord for me, and the issue is settled."

If people come to you when you are in the middle of a battle with sickness and say, "God showed me that you will roll over and die," you should shake your head and say, "That's not the word of the Lord for me." If you get a surprising diagnosis and a gloomy prognosis after medical tests and biopsies, then get the word of the Lord on the issue! What is God saying to you?

People may tell you with authority that you will fail financially, or they may apologize and tell you that they're going to shut down the plant where you work. You just go to your prayer closet and pray, "God, please give me a word so I can stand." If God tells you, "You won't lose your job," then don't be surprised if they pass you by when they start down the row passing out the pink slips! Folks may look at you and say, "Wait a minute, this isn't fair! I've been here 12 years and you've only been here 5 years!" They don't know that the Lord says, "When I see the blood, I see someone standing in covenant. When I see someone stand where I told them to stand and do what I told them to do, I will cause calamity to 'pass over' them."

God's Word Will Stand

God honors obedience, faith, and hope—even though it involves the simple but unusual act of throwing some lamb's blood on the doorposts and lintel of your house (as Moses and all the Israelites did in the land of Pharaoh in Exodus 12:7). God said, "I will pass over." When he sent the angel of death across the land God changes conditions and circumstances for those who will stand in faith. Folks may send you dandelions, but God will change every dandelion into an instrument of His purposes for your life.

You may face an entire book of rules and regulations that says your situation is hopeless. If you hear God's word to the contrary, then watch Him blind people to the rules and regulations, which do not have the authority to contradict His will. For some reason, they will find themselves saying, "I don't even know why I'm doing this. I don't know why I'm accepting this application late." You will just smile and say, "I know."

In every situation, my prayer to God is, "Give me a word, Lord. Just give me a word, and I'll be ready to stand." Once I receive that word from the heavenly realm of the Spirit, then I put it in my heart. Jesus said:

> *...Whosoever shall say unto this mountain, Be thou removed, and be thou cast into the sea; and shall not doubt in his heart, but shall believe that those things which he saith shall come to pass; he shall have whatsoever he saith. Therefore I say unto you, What things soever ye desire, when ye pray, believe that ye receive them, and ye shall have them* (Mark 11:23-24).

Take God's Word and hide it in your heart. Get it down into your inner being. Every time the enemy comes along, just tell him, "It is written. Thus saith the Lord." Those nearby may look at you like you're crazy and say, "Look around you, man!" But you can simply say, "I can't look at the crisis or the circumstances; faith refuses to look at the circumstances as the final word. Faith only looks to God, for His Word is final."

"So then faith cometh by hearing, and hearing by the word of God" (Rom. 10:17). Faith always embraces the Word. Faith does not "twist God's arm"; it simply fights against everything that exalts itself against the knowledge of God. It brings into captivity every thought to the obedience of that Word.

We're not talking about "faith in my faith," we're talking about having faith in God.

It's Not Your Job...

Trust actually goes beyond faith. I've come to understand that my faith consists of simply relying and reclining on the Lord and expecting Him to do what only He can do. I used to teach swimming at a summer camp when I was a youth. A grown lady came down to the pool one year who did not know how to swim. We always started the swimming lessons by teaching our students how to float, so I told this lady, "Okay, lay out on the water." Everything went well as long as I helped keep her afloat. But once I stepped away, she would sink, only to get back up choking and coughing.

No matter how many times I'd say, "Just lay out on the water and float," she would lay out and promptly sink like a rock! I stepped back and watched her one time as I said, "Now lay out on the water— *everybody* floats." This woman was a bit overweight; and since body fat is very buoyant, it stood to reason her extra pounds should have amounted to a natural "life preserver" for her. It should have been almost impossible for her to sink, yet whenever I told the woman to lay out on the water, she obeyed and promptly sank under the surface! Then I saw what she was doing.

"Watch me," I told her. I laid out on the water and gritted my teeth, knotted my hands into tight fists, and turned my toenails down—and immediately sank like a rock too. She nodded in relief and said, "Oh, you can't float either!"

"Oh yeah, I can float," I told her. "Listen to me: In every person's body there is what is called 'buoyancy.' Only one out of every hundred people cannot float at all. *It is not your responsibility to hold yourself up on the water!* If you will lay out on the water and rest, then buoyancy will come into play and the water itself will hold you up."

At first, when I said, "Lay out on the water and relax," I could see her hands tighten up again, so I said, "Relax." I felt kind of like a dentist telling someone in his dentist's chair to "relax." Nevertheless, I told her, "Relax, now lay out on the water." I let go of her and she went down a little bit and then came back up. Once she relaxed, she began to float on the water.

God Will Make It Happen

Come unto Me, all ye that labour and are heavy laden, and I will give you rest. Take My yoke upon you, and learn of Me; for I am meek and lowly in heart: and ye shall find rest unto your souls. For My yoke is easy, and My burden is light (Matthew 11:28-30).

Jesus says to each of us in this walk of faith, "It's not up to you to make it happen. It's not up to you to wonder whether or not faith worked or didn't work. You'll find rest unto your souls if you come unto Me, for My yoke is easy and My burden is light." When you first lay out and rest on the water, it may seem like you are going under for just a minute, then the water will hold you up. That is all God wants to do in your life. What is patience for? Patience gives you the strength and supernatural energy to stand in divine grace while you are waiting for a thing to transfer itself from the spirit realm to the natural realm.

Just as money is a means of exchange in the natural realm, so faith is a means of exchange in the spiritual realm. We receive things in the spirit realm through the medium of faith as

God brings us from level to level, from glory to glory, and from faith to faith. He is calling you to minister according to the portion of faith that is in you. At the same time He is increasing your faith (see Rom. 12:3,6; 2 Cor. 10:15).

Faith is like a seed that becomes planted in the earth. The emphasis is not on how big your faith is, but on the potential resident in the faith that God has given to you. He says, "If you will just sow it in good ground, that thing will begin to grow and blossom until you will be able to push over any problem in your life."

Affliction Follows Revelation

You must have a word from the Lord because it is through faith and patience that you receive the promises of God. "But call to remembrance the former days, in which, after ye were illuminated, ye endured a great fight of afflictions" (Heb. 10:32). Do you see the pattern in this verse? First we are enlightened, then we endure affliction. It is clear that the assault of the enemy *comes because of the Word.*

Every time God has unveiled and unfolded a secret, a mystery, or a revelation to me, affliction and assault also seemed to be close behind as I broke through to that new level of revelation and clarity. I think that as soon as you and I "get it," the enemy says, "Now let's see if you've really got it." Remember the parable of the sower in Matthew 13. Every time seed is sown, the enemy is there watching. He is like a bird who waits patiently for any opportunity to swoop in and snatch it away. If you spring up immediately with joy and say, "I got it! I got it!" he says, "Oh really? Here is some tribulation and persecution. Let's see if you've *really* got it."

In 1985, I felt I had heard from God on a matter, so I began to pray with leaders in the church about leaving my "tent-making" job to come on as a full-time pastor of our young church body. At the beginning of 1986, I weighed about 240 pounds, but by March, my weight dropped to 190 pounds, and then to 185 pounds. In only 90 days I had lost 50-to-60 pounds!

We had already planned to go into full-time ministry, but my health and body weight dropped so low that I began to experience severe chest pain and vision problems. One day I actually woke up to discover that I was temporarily blind! The enemy had assaulted my eyes, and although I tried my best to get up and go to work, I couldn't make it. My wife, Theresa, asked, "What do you want me to do?" I mumbled, "Take me to a specialist."

I was diagnosed as having uveitis, a severe infection of the eye. The doctor said, "There's probably some internal problems, but if it clears up just let it go." (Now *that's* an encouraging statement!) The infection cleared up and we let it go, but the weight condition didn't improve. I started to get weaker, and I finally went to a doctor for some tests. He said I was basically healthy, but then he said, "I don't understand this weight loss. I didn't like the sound that I'm hearing in this lung. Go get an X-ray." Then during the physical exam, he found a lump on the outside of one of my testicles. (Talk about breaking into new levels....) He said, "I want you to go to the hospital and have an X-ray done on your chest, and then you need to go to a specialist and have the testicle checked."

As soon as the X-rays were examined later that day, my doctor called the house and said, "Tell LaFayette when he comes home from work that I want him to go to the hospital *now*!" When I got to the hospital that evening, the doctors began to run a whole battery of tests. Then I underwent two surgical biopsies to find out what was happening. They found out that I had a rare disease called "sarcoidosis." It produces malignant growths all over the body. Sometimes it even produces them in the eyes, and sometimes in the heart. If it strikes the heart it can kill you instantly. The doctors found tumors, or growths, in my liver and lungs, and they thought the lump on my testicle was a sarcoma as well, but they weren't sure.

A lung biopsy confirmed the presence of a diseased nodule in my lungs, so they started treating me with drugs. At one point, one of the doctors said, "One of the members of your church told me you were planning to quit your job." I said, "That's right." Then he pointed a finger in my face and said, "Don't quit your job. I know the company that you work for, and they have great benefits. Now we can bring this disease you have into remission. But it may reoccur at any time, and this disease has usually become a lifelong battle for the people I've seen with it." Then he said, "I don't know what your prognosis will be. I know we can try to bring it into remission, but we don't know when it's going to spring back up again."

Then he turned even more serious and said, "We think this disease is what is in your testicle, but we'll have to do a biopsy to be sure," and that's what they did. I said, "What happens if you find out that this thing in the testicle isn't the same thing? Why don't we just assume that it is?" He said, "No, we can't do that. What if it's cancerous or something like that? We would do you a disservice." So I asked him again, "What if you find out that it's not the same stuff?" He said, "Well, we'll just have to extract the testicle."

Now this statement might not mean a lot to my female readers, but when you start telling a brother you're going to cut his stuff off, you have captured his full attention! I came before the congregation and said, "Church, it's time to pray. If you haven't ever prayed before, it's time to pray now."

The doctors tried to schedule this dreaded biopsy surgery three or four times without success because my temperature was fluctuating all the time. Finally the doctors asked, "What are you going to do with this job?" I said, "God's told me to go into the ministry fulltime."

Almost immediately there was another all-out assault on my physical body. I was confined to a bed in the hospital in the same month Integrity Music put out a praise tape with the song that says, "I am the Lord that healeth thee, I am the Lord Your healer. I sent My word and healed your disease. I am the Lord your Healer" ("I Am the Lord That Healeth Thee" Don Moen © 1986 Hosanna Music/Maranatha Music). My wife brought that tape to the hospital, and I listened to it around the clock on my headset. (Every other day she brought in replacement batteries.) I read the Word and had that anointed music coming into my head all day long. To this day, I probably know every song and every music sequence on that tape.

Meanwhile, a woman prophesied, "The pastor is under tremendous assault, but it's a sanctified time." Theresa brought a tape of the prophecy to me in the hospital, and when I asked her how the service went, she said, "It was fantastic. Revea told me to give you this." I listened to the prophecy tape in amazement as this woman said, "This sickness is not unto death, but this is a sanctified time. God is going to bring you through it!" Then she charged the men of the church to rise up and pray for me from 6-to-7:00 a.m., and the men responded by rising and committing to pray for me each day at 6:00 in the morning for a month. (This daily prayer time continues to this day.)

When I was released from the hospital, the prognosis was the same: "We can bring him into remission, but we don't know when the condition will occur again." For nearly a year, all the medical people said, "Don't quit your job because this is an expensive disease. We don't know if it will reoccur, and the church can't bear this burden." We talked about it, and we prayed about it. Predictably, when we checked on purchasing individual health insurance policies, they said, "We can insure you, but if this disease reoccurs, you're on your own because it was a preexisting condition."

The enemy will assault you in your mind every time you dare to reach for more in God. That is why you urgently need faith and patience to endure. Once God has instructed you to do a thing, the enemy will unleash everything he has on that level in an effort to make you fall back in fear or discouragement.

I am not moved by a lot of the stuff I hear and see anymore. It's not that I'm cold, but I have already faced that demon before. I know what it is like to have a demon come and sit on your bed and say, "I'm going to take your life." I also know what is it like to have God send someone in who will declare to you in your discouragement, "This affliction is not unto death, for you will live and not die!"

People look at me today and say, "Well, you're a pretty big man now, Brother LaFayette. You don't look sick now." I tell them, "That's is only because of God's grace. You're looking at the fruit of the fervent prayers of the saints mixed with faith and the power of God. Together, we make an unbeatable team and we break our way into new levels of God's glory."

On January 1, 1987, I walked back into the package delivery firm where I had been working and passed all the physicals. My health was restored. I met with my supervisor on January 2nd, and he said, "You are scheduled to come back to work since you passed all the tests." That was when I gave him the signed resignation notice I had written six months ago and said, "I'm sorry, but the people of God need me more than the delivery trucks now." I made the transition never looked back. It is through faith and patience that you inherit the promise.

The Reward of Reproach

Cast not away therefore your confidence, which hath great recompense of reward. For ye have need of patience, that, after ye have done the will of God, ye might receive the promise (Hebrews 10:35-36).

The will of God is that you stand up against the assault of the enemy. At every turn in your journey to greater maturity and intimacy with God, the enemy will try to entangle you with the enticements and activities of the world as you begin to live out the things you've received from God and His Word. These include the alluring power of deceitfulness and riches, which he uses to choke the Word out of you. And many times, as in my case, the assault may be made directly on your life.

When God's Word lands in "good ground" (the open and obedient heart of a true believer) that has been thoroughly purged, then His Word sinks a root deep into the soil and produces 30-, 60-, and 100-fold!

But call to remembrance the former days, in which, after ye were illuminated, ye endured a great fight of afflictions; partly, whilst ye were made a gazingstock both by reproaches and afflictions; and partly, whilst ye became companions of them that were so used (Hebrews 10:32-33).

To be "made a gazingstock" means to "be made an example." Sometimes God seems to "hang us out" in vulnerable positions as an example for the world, and I don't know why He does it. Can you imagine yourself locked into one of those old public stocks they had in colonial New England? Your punishment would be open to everybody. Picture yourself bent over in total vulnerability with your head and hands locked in place while everybody passing by said "that person really messed up!"

The Book of Hebrews is saying to us, "Sometimes it may seem like you are in this same situation. You will feel like Samson, who was put on public display in the center of his enemies' city to grind out corn in humiliation."

Hebrews 10:33 says "ye were made a gazingstock *both by reproaches and afflictions.*" That is where loneliness comes in. Like Christ before us (see Mt. 27:46), we sometimes cry, "My God, My God, why has Thou forsaken me?" (I pray that you never get to that place.) I remember times when I broke into new levels through reproaches and by affliction. If I hadn't known His promise to "never leave thee nor forsake me" (Heb. 13:5), I would have thought God had "gone away." I didn't feel one ounce of the presence of the Lord. I didn't feel any anointing. It seemed like God just "wasn't around."

I had no tangible proof of His presence, and my senses were useless in my search for Him. The only thing I could hold on to was His Word: "I will never leave thee, nor forsake thee" (Heb. 13:5). I would have been afraid and dismayed, but I had His Word on the matter: "And the Lord, He it is that doth go before thee; He will be with thee, He will not fail thee, neither forsake thee: fear not, neither be dismayed" (Deut. 31:8). If I had not had that divine word that says, "Lo, I am with you alway, even unto the end of the world..." (Mt. 28:20b), then I would have given up. "I had fainted, unless I had believed to see the goodness of the Lord in the land of the living" (Ps. 27:13).

Sometimes when we look back and see how God hung Jesus up between heaven and earth, we feel like we've been hung up there too. Yet the writer of Hebrews says:

> *...After ye were illuminated, ye endured a great fight of afflictions; partly, whilst ye were made a gazingstock both by reproaches and afflictions; and partly, whilst ye became companions of them that were so used. For ye had compassion of me in my bonds, and took joyfully the spoiling of your goods, knowing in yourselves that ye have in heaven a better and an enduring substance* (Hebrews 10:32b-34).

Heaven is filled with the presence of God. It is His dwelling place and the seat of His rule and government, the habitation of our better and enduring substance. God said, "You will discover that once you understand My reign, My rule, My presence, and My government, that anything that you lose in your earthly life can be marked a 'temporary loss.' For you will regain it again under My righteous government, rule, and authority."

Paul said, "Yea doubtless, and I count all things but loss for the excellency of the knowledge of Christ Jesus my Lord: for whom I have suffered the loss of all things, and do count them but dung, that I may win Christ" (Phil. 3:8). He was saying he counted his reputation, resumé, family lineage, and nationality as mere "dung" in comparison to winning Christ.

Cast not away therefore your confidence, which hath great recompence of reward. For ye have need of patience, that, after ye have done the will of God, ye might receive the promise. For yet a little while, and he that shall come will come, and will not tarry. Now the just shall live by faith: but if any man draw back, my soul shall have no pleasure in him. But we are not of them who draw back unto perdition; but of them that believe to the saving of the soul (Hebrews 10:35-39).

It is essential that you have confidence when you are breaking into new levels in God. You have to be confident that if God calls you higher, then He will bring you up to that level. Don't let the devil tell you he will kill you before you obtain it; he simply has *no say in the matter*! Keep your confidence in God.

Chapter 6

Transformation by Revelation

Grow in Understanding

God loves babies, but He also expects them to grow and move on to the next stage some day. In First Peter 2:2, the apostle Peter compared new believers to babes in Christ who desire the sincere milk of the Word. The last two verses of Hebrews 5 say that spiritual babes are unskillful in the Word of righteousness. That is why it is important for you to move from being a babe to what is called "a child in God"— and beyond.

Who Am I?

First John 2 says, "I write unto you, *little children*, because your sins are forgiven you...I write unto you, *little children*, because ye have known the Father" (1 Jn. 2:12-13b). A believer at the "child of God" level understands his or her rights in Christ, that he is forgiven and has the righteousness of God in Christ Jesus. "Children" understand that they have been justified and elected to the things of God. A "child" in the faith has begun to understand the elementary principles of the Word of God found in Hebrews 6:1-2, including repentance from dead works, faith toward God, doctrines of baptisms, laying on of hands, resurrection of the dead, and eternal judgment.

From the "child" level you press upward to the level of "young man" in the faith. First John says, "I write unto you, young men, because ye have overcome the wicked one ... I have written unto you, young men, because ye are strong, and the word of God abideth in you, and ye have overcome the wicked one" (1 Jn. 2:13b,14b).

Believers at the "young man" stage have begun to understand who the devil is, what the devil has, and what the devil can do. They also understand who God is, what God has, and what God can do. Finally, they understand who they are, what they have, and what they can do.

The Word of God praises "young men" (it is really referring to a stage of development that crosses gender lines) because these believers can *overcome the devil* in their newfound identity and knowledge! This is a vital function of this stage of development. These people meet the devil with an advantage because they understand who they are, what they have in Christ, and what they can do in His name. The Word says, "Ye are of God, little children, and have overcome them: because greater is He that is in you, than he that is in the world" (1 Jn. 4:4).

Even though "little children" have begun to understand that the Greater One is in them, those believers at the "young

man" stage not only have the head knowledge of that principle, they have also become overcomers. There is a big difference between saying you are an "overcomer" and actually
overcoming the enemy as a believer in the "young man"
stage. A lot of people can quote, "Greater is He that is in me
than he that is in the world" (see 1 Jn. 4:4). Yet the moment "he
that is in the world" comes around, most of them quiver, shrink
down, and fall back under the pressure of evil opposition.

These people can fight demons when they're "out there"
somewhere where they can't be seen, and their presence isn't
felt. But when one come close with their name on it, these
children of God shrink back and become "as small grasshop-
pers" in the eyes of devilish principalities, powers, and do-
minions (see Num. 13:13). "Young men," on the other hand,
meet the devil with advantage and overcome him because the
Word of God abides in them.

Who Are We?

"I have written unto you, fathers, because ye have known
Him that is from the beginning" (1 Jn. 2:14a; see also 1 Jn.
2:13a). John repeats this statement twice to emphasize the
chief strength and characteristic of spiritual fathers. Spiritual
fathers seem to have a sense of eternal destiny and the purposes of God. Paul wrote to the church at Corinth:

*For though ye have ten thousand instructors in Christ,
yet have ye not many fathers: for in Christ Jesus I have
begotten you through the gospel. Wherefore I beseech
you, be ye followers of me. For this cause have I sent unto
you Timotheus, who is my beloved son, and faithful in*

*the Lord, who shall bring you into remembrance of my
ways which be in Christ, as I teach every where in
every church* (1 Corinthians 4:15-17).

A father is one who reproduces after his kind, a mature
spiritual leader to whom God can entrust His treasure, which
is the Body of Christ.

In the Old Testament, God raised up Deborah, a self-
described "mother in Israel" to rouse His sleepy people and
deliver them from an oppressive king. In the Church of Jesus
Christ, God is raising up "fathers" in the faith as foretold by
the prophet Malachi, who ended the Old Covenant record
with the prophetic words:

*Behold, I will send you Elijah the prophet before the
coming of the great and dreadful day of the Lord: and
he shall turn the heart of the fathers to the children,
and the heart of the children to their fathers, lest I
come and smite the earth with a curse* (Malachi 4:5-6).

Paul was a father in the faith and one of our greatest exam-
ples of spiritual fatherhood. If you want to understand his
heart, just read his letters to his spiritual son, Timothy. Paul
said of his "adopted" son:

*For I have no man likeminded, who will naturally care
for your state. For all seek their own, not the things
which are Jesus Christ's. But ye know the proof of him,
that, as a son with the father, he hath served with me in
the gospel* (Philippians 2:20-22).

Timothy was a spiritual son who was born out of Paul's experience in ministry as a *father in the faith.*

Corporate Identity

It was Paul who revealed the next level of maturity in God's order—the level of the "perfect man." In his letter to the church at Ephesus, he wrote:

> *And He gave some, apostles; and some, prophets; and some, evangelists; and some, pastors and teachers; for the perfecting of the saints, for the work of the ministry, for the edifying of the body of Christ: till we all come in the unity of the faith, and of the knowledge of the Son of God, unto a perfect man, unto the measure of the stature of the fulness of Christ* (Ephesians 4:11-14).

The "perfect man" is a "corporate" state of maturity. It is not something we achieve alone as with the first four levels; we become "perfected" together. As we grow and move through the various levels of God individually, a crucial transformation takes place. We gradually come to the place where we're not so concerned about "me" becoming perfected. We are more concerned about "us," the Church, the Body of Christ. Our vision expands too. Our focus moves beyond the "spiritual babes" stage where we ravenously consumed every Christian teaching tape, book, and magazine article we could find. We still "eat" spiritual food, but it is no longer our exclusive focus.

We are no longer children trying to find out "who we are" in Christ. Nor are we "young men" primarily motivated to "fight the devil." We still continue to be "spiritual fathers," but we can no longer be preoccupied with giving birth and taking responsibility to know the eternal purposes of God. You cannot be "perfected" without me, and I cannot be perfected without you. The "perfect man" always speaks of corporateness.

This pattern extends all the way back to the Jewish patriarchs, judges, and prophets of the Old Testament. The Book of Hebrews talks about all the great people in the "faith hall of fame" in the eleventh chapter, including Daniel, Samson, Japheth, Abraham, Jacob, Abel, and Enoch:

And these all, having obtained a good report through faith, received not the promise: God having provided some better thing for us, that they without us should not be made perfect (Hebrews 11:39-40).

That means they couldn't be perfected without us because perfection is a corporate state of being. The Body of Christ will only be perfected to the degree that everybody in it gets perfected. That is God's desire. He want to help us all "grow up" into "the measure of the stature of the fulness of Christ" (Eph. 4:13).

Glorified Bride

The last level of maturity involves the "Glorified Man," when we have all made ourselves ready as the Bride of Christ. Then He shall appear, and we shall see Him and be like Him; "for we shall see Him as He is" (1 Jn. 3:2). That is the visible appearing of the Lord Jesus Christ. The "Glorified Man" is actually the Body of Christ fully prepared and perfected, without spot or wrinkle or any such thing. In that moment, as we behold Him, together we will be changed. Mortality will put on immortality, and corruption will put on incorruption:

Behold, I shew you a mystery; We shall not all sleep, but we shall all be changed, in a moment, in the twinkling of an eye, at the last trump: for the trumpet shall sound, and the dead shall be raised incorruptible, and we shall be changed. For this corruptible must put on incorruption, and this mortal must put on immortality (1 Corinthians 15:51-53).

It is our destiny to "be glorified." In fact, God's Word says, "...the creature waiteth for the manifestation of the sons of God ... For we know that the whole creation groaneth and travaileth in pain together until now" (Rom. 8:19,22). God is waiting for the bride of Christ to perfect herself by the Spirit and by the Word.

One Step at a Time

The Bible says, "The entrance of Thy words giveth light" (Ps. 119:130a). How? "Wherewithal shall a young man cleanse his way? by taking heed thereto according to Thy word. With my whole heart have I sought Thee: O let me not wander from Thy commandments. Thy word have I hid in mine heart, that I might not sin against Thee" (Ps. 119:9-11).

At each level there are progressive steps leading from that level to the next, and you don't step straight from the floor to the platform. You have to go up a step at a time.

Paul wrote to the church at Galatia about some of the hindrances believers encounter when they decide to press on and grow. Paul had done a great job of delivering the gospel to these people, and he wanted them to hold on to it. Then someone came along while they were running their race and said, "You guys are not keeping the law. You've been worshiping on the wrong day and eating the wrong foods. Some of you aren't even circumcised!" (see Gal. 3:1)

The Galatians' progress toward maturity began to slow down when someone preached a different gospel from the authentic gospel. Paul declared early in his letter to the church, "But though we, or an angel from heaven, preach any other gospel unto you than that which we have preached unto you, let him be accursed" (Gal. 1:8). The Greek word translated "accursed" is *anathama*. It means "to be brought to not, to put away." The Galatians were caught in a battle between man's religious reasoning and God's reasoning, between a false gospel of works and a true gospel of grace. Are you going to obey God or man's reasoning?

Whenever you decide to move upward or out in the things of God, don't be surprised if people begin to look at you and bring man's reasoning into the picture. They may tell you that you've become too radical and fanatical. They will either say "It doesn't take all that effort," *or* that you are "not doing enough."

Paul told the believers in Galatia "...I neither received it [the gospel] of man, neither was I taught it, but by revelation of Jesus Christ" (Gal. 1:12). The only way you can break through certain spiritual levels of growth is by revelation. Victory only comes when God shines His light on a situation. The Greek word for "revelation," which appears throughout the New Testament, is *apokalupsis*. It means "the uncovering or the unveiling of a thing." This meaning goes beyond mere "disclosure" to the "interpretation" of a mystery. When God unveils and discloses, He shines a light on the truth making it apparent to you along with a proper interpretation of it. That is called "understanding."

An Unfolding Revelation

"Wisdom is the principle thing; therefore get wisdom: and with all thy getting get understanding" (Prov. 4:7). Paul told the church at Ephesus, "I'm praying that God will give you the Spirit of wisdom and of revelation in the knowledge of Him, that the eyes of your understanding would be enlightened ... because all levels are coming up into Him, that we might grow up in the measure of the fulness of Christ into the perfect man" (from the "LaFayette Scales version" of Ephesians 1:16-18;4:13). God isn't interested in people growing up into LaFayette's doctrine— or Rhema Bible Training Center's doctrine—no; we are growing up into the measure of the stature of the fullness of Christ.

Every advance to a new level in God requires a fresh and clear revelation of the Lord Jesus Christ. People grow to the proportion of their revelation of Christ Jesus and no further. The only way to grow and move on in Christ is to understand and embrace more of Him today than you did yesterday. It is possible to walk in Christ for 5 years, 10 years, or 25 years, and just know Him as Savior. The problem is: He has much more to give us, and His dreams for us are too wonderful to be fulfilled by merely "standing at the entrance" to His Kingdom. He urges us to climb higher and press into Him. When we do, we glorify Him.

If somebody pointed you out and said, "Stand up and testify, sir." You could say, "Well, 20 years ago, I got saved," and that would be it. That's a wonderful beginning, but where is the fruit? Where are the multiplied talents that you have "invested" in this life to return to the Master 5-, 10-, and 100-fold? It is also possible to stop at another milestone and know Jesus Christ as the "baptizer with the Holy Ghost."

"Stand up and testify, brother." "Twenty years ago, I was saved, but I didn't have any power. Then I met Jesus the baptizer with the Holy Ghost. I went down to the altar, and I bowed my knees. I tarried and I shouted, and when my shoes were full of sweat and my shirt was soaking wet, I broke through and I got my blessing." The simple truth is that God wants you and I to be conformed in the image of His son (Rom. 8:29). As long as there is something in our lives that still needs conformed, we need more of Him and have no business "stopping to build an altar to our accomplishments."

The power of Paul's teaching flowed from the fact that he taught "by revelation of Jesus Christ," and not man. Teaching is important. Instruction and discipleship is important, but we must allow the Holy Spirit to make the things of God real to us. When something "jumps off" the pages of the Bible and leaps into your heart, then you know God has shined the light of revelation on it. When Scripture becomes a reality to you, it is through revelation by the Holy Spirit.

Divine Credentials

When God stamps a thing in your heart, you can say "I've got it." Then you won't have to teach like the scribes and Pharisees, who effectively said, "This person says this, and this professor says that. This seminary teaches this, and both Kenneth Hagin and Fred Price said that. And you know Myles Munroe says this." No, you will be able to declare with confidence, "But God said...."

In the last day, that great day of the feast, Jesus stood and cried, saying, If any man thirst, let him come unto Me, and drink. He that believeth on Me, as the scripture hath said, out of his belly shall flow rivers of living water ... Then came the officers to the chief priests and Pharisees; and they said unto them, Why have ye not brought Him? The officers answered, Never man spake like this man (John 7:37-38,45-46).

That is what made Jesus so different from the teachers of His generation. They said, "Never man spake like this man." When everyone else was busy quoting other rabbis and teachers, this upstart from Galilee dared to say, "I am only telling you the things I got from My Father. I saw Him doing it, and that is why I'm doing it. I heard Him say it, so now I'm saying it to you" (see Jn. 5:17-24).

Paul carefully separated his "real credentials" received by revelation in the Spirit from those earned in the schools and systems of man:

For ye have heard of my conversation in time past in the Jews' religion, how that beyond measure I persecuted the church of God, and wasted it: and profited in the Jews' religion above many my equals in mine own nation, being more exceedingly zealous of the traditions of my fathers. But when it pleased God, who separated me from my mother's womb, and called me by His grace, to reveal His Son in me... (Galatians 1:13-16).

In other words, Paul was out there doing what he thought was good, but it wasn't God. The only way we get saved is when the Son is *revealed* in us. The Holy Spirit has to unveil the Son to our darkened hearts and minds. Otherwise, we will just play religious games and miss God totally. What a shame it would be to come to the end of your life after doing a lot of "good stuff" that simply "wasn't God's stuff." In the judgment, you would find out that God never knew you!

Revelation, Not Religion

It is too easy to do "religious stuff" instead of God's will. Religion is man's collection of "nots." It consists of observing commands like "touch not, do not, handle not, dress not, and go not." I know it is difficult for a believer to know how to dress, where to go, what to taste, what to drink, and what to let alone. We could spend so much time majoring on the "don'ts" that we would never get around to "doing the 'dos.' "

Religion is easy, but it doesn't give life. I could tell all the ministers at my church to put on collars. I could tell all the women to line up so we could measure their hemlines before we let them into the building. We could all decide that would be more holy if we all wore head coverings in public. In fact, we could decide that the surest way to be saved is to dress and act in some stupid way so we'll be "different" from the world. We could also go the opposite direction and substitute piety and dignity (if you will) for an outward display of holiness. "We've got to get this thing dignified." The problem is that salvation is found in no other place, action, or thing than in the shed blood, sacrificial death, and resurrection of Jesus Christ.

Paul was saying, "I was zealous. I was above my equals. I wasted the church. (Paul was zealous in his *religion*.) But the thing that turned me around wasn't an argument, persuasion, or teaching. My salvation came when God, in the fullness of time, began to reveal His Son in me. Once His Son was revealed in me, I changed."

Many people think that by creating "more rules" they can change folks. The truth is that rules only put people in a box. It is like putting a muzzle on a Doberman pinscher—you aren't taking the bite out of him, you're just temporarily restraining his actions. God is not interested in "restraining actions" in our lives. He is saying, "I want to change your nature. I want to take the bite right out you so I can remove the muzzle of the law and release you to walk up and down the street arrayed with dignity as I always intended." The law is for the lawless. When we come to Christ, we begin to understand that the only way we change is by revelation. Christ must first be revealed to us, and then we will change.

Paul said, "But when it pleased God, who separated me from my mother's womb, and called me by His grace, to reveal His Son in me, that I might preach Him among the heathen; immediately I conferred not with flesh and blood" (Gal. 1:15-16). When you get a revelation, it is best that you just hold onto that truth for a while. Don't run off to share it with everybody. Give the Holy Ghost some time to hover over that thing and reveal it within you before somebody comes along to throw water on it and rob you of God's truth.

Nurture Your Revelation

Whenever you get on fire because God has shown you something, it is almost comical the way someone will come along and tell you, "That ain't right! I don't see that. That just ain't the way Kenneth Copeland teaches it!" They'll just dump water and sand all over your fire, and in the process they might get you to think, "My goodness, I thought God showed me something—I guess I was wrong." When God speaks to you, you will be changed. His Word will make you readjust things in your life. It will give you a new walk, and help you break into a new level. When God does something inside of you, you don't have to go run to men. The fruits of His truth in your life will tell the story soon enough.

Revelation is progressive and ongoing. It is *never* stagnant! Paul said, "When I received the revelation of God's Son, immediately I conferred not with flesh and blood." The Spirit of God, the Holy Ghost, is also called the Spirit of Truth. If you keep holding a thought, a Scripture, or an understanding up to God and say, "Lord, I want to teach this," He will begin to deal with your heart. He will separate the true from the false, and He will begin to stack the revelation line upon line, precept upon precept, here a little, there a little (see Is. 28:10-11).

If a thing is true, then you will begin to find that the truth you've received runs from cover to cover in God's Word, from Genesis to Revelation, and "from Dan to Beersheba." The truths of God are consistent, because He does not contradict Himself.

Neither went I up to Jerusalem to them which were apostles before me; but I went into Arabia, and returned again unto Damascus. Then after three years I went up to Jerusalem to see Peter, and abode with him fifteen days. But other of the apostles saw I none, save James the Lord's brother (Galatians 1:17-19).

Paul met with the apostles in Jerusalem only *after* he had received a direct revelation of Jesus Christ in the wilderness. Why? Paul was destined to have a different assignment from his Jewish brethren. God had to totally separate Paul from the old ways of thinking to plant His purposes in him without the contamination of "Jerusalem and Judaism-centered" thought.

God sent Peter to go to the Jews first and then to the Greeks with a basic assignment to open the door of the gospel to the Jews. But Paul had a direct revelation that led him to break with the status quo. "And I went up by revelation, and communicated unto them that gospel which I preach among the Gentiles..." (Gal. 2:2). This mission was a little bit different from what the boys in Jerusalem were used to. When God led Paul to the desert wastes of Arabia for three years, Paul didn't spend his time out there just trying to get "some new thing." He diligently talked with the Lord, dialogued, and searched the scrolls (the Scriptures).

What about you? Do you realize that the same God who revealed His Son in you as Savior can also reveal His Son in you as truth? God longs for you to develop sensitivity to the Spirit of truth. Every level of maturity that you break into requires greater degrees of sensitivity to the revelation of the knowledge of Him. Paul wasn't praying empty words when he prayed for the believers at Ephesus—he had personal knowledge of what he was talking about when he prayed:

That the God of our Lord Jesus Christ, the Father of glory, may give unto you the spirit of wisdom and revelation in the knowledge of Him: the eyes of your understanding being enlightened; that ye may know what is the hope of His calling, and what the riches of the glory of His inheritance in the saints, and what is the exceeding greatness of His power to us-ward who believe, according to the working of His mighty power (Ephesians 1:17-19).

Paul told the Galatians, "Then *fourteen years after* I went up again to Jerusalem with Barnabas, and took Titus with me also" (Gal. 2:1). Would you be willing to wait for 14 years while the Holy Spirit planted a revelation in your heart? Paul did, and he ended up turning the world upside down with that truth. Some folks hear something one day and want to preach it tomorrow! Let the Holy Ghost hover over it. I tell our ministers, "If it is true, it will wait. It will keep until God is ready to release it in you."

Maturation Takes Time

Look at the Old Testament patriarchs and the disciples of Jesus. They all had to wait. They had to "pay their dues" and allow God to do some work in them before they could launch out on a mission. The disciples had to walk with Jesus for three years. Then He said, "You still aren't ready. *Wait* here in Jerusalem." He taught them for another 40 days after He was resurrected, only to tell them again, "You still aren't ready. *Wait* 10 more days." After the Holy Ghost came and baptized them with fire, then they were ready to preach and to minister. Don't be deceived—it takes time for God to reveal His Son in us.

"Paul, he was a religious guy. He sat at the feet of Gamaliel. He had a lot of knowledge and insight. Surely he should have gotten it just like that." No, God takes His time burning His revelation into us because of our own weaknesses, and because of the intensity of opposition we will face when we walk out the revelation. Paul spent three years in the Arabian desert receiving the revelation, followed by a 15-day visit with church leaders in Jerusalem to explain the vision. Then, after 14 years of powerful ministry with signs and wonders among the Gentiles, Paul returned to Jerusalem "by revelation," taking Barnabas and Titus with him. He once again rehearsed to the church leaders there the gospel he preached among the Gentiles because Judaizers had sown strife over his work among non-Jews. The Jewish leaders could not understand how the Gentiles were being blessed without being circumcised. They met at Jerusalem and dialogued about some of these matters.

Paul didn't go up to Jerusalem or out into the mission field in his own strength or by man's doctrine. He went up armed only with what God had revealed to him supernaturally. The fruit of his divine commission convinced James, Peter, and John that God had conferred on Paul and Barnabus an apostolic call to the Gentiles, so they blessed and approved their work.

At every level you break into, God will command you and demand that you *learn a lesson*. At on every level, there will be a fresh and new unveiling, an unfolding of God's nature and knowledge within you. You will sense a "light turn on" inside your being, revealing new knowledge of Him on that level. At every point in your Christian walk, God is out to reveal Himself to you.

Chapter 7

Persistence in the Face of Resistance

...False brethren unawares brought in, who came in privily to spy out our liberty which we have in Christ Jesus, that they might bring us into bondage: to whom we gave place by subjection, no, not for an hour; that the truth of the gospel might continue with you (Galatians 2:4-5).

Any time you begin to move in the revelation that God gives you, you will always run into people who will want to put restraints on your message and ministry! You can count on it. These "restraints" are tools of bondage, and bondage just isn't a part of the plan and the purposes of God!

God Is Not Sectarian

It is the nature of men and women who have not received a revelation themselves to try to attach "additional comments and insights" to your revelation that the Spirit of God just didn't say. To "be bound" means to close off, tie up, and restrain a thing. That is what the "false brethren" wanted to do with Paul's message and mission to the Gentiles.

Now God is a God of order. He is a God of *fusion*, not confusion. God is supernaturally fusing people together, saying, "You have the same vision and the same purpose." We still have to learn how to yield to one another. The enemy's greatest attempts to infiltrate and bring bondage are directed at individuals and groups in the Church who have the revelation of the Lord for that season. The devil wants to neutralize people who have a sensitive ear for what the Spirit of God is saying. Our greatest vulnerability comes when God begins to move again, because we are forced to move beyond our previous revelation to a new level—and most of us just don't want to go when that happens.

God never has fixed His operations so that one group will always have or know "everything" that God is doing. (He knows we would get proud and sectarian—just look at Church history.) We might begin to call ourselves the "true Church of Jesus Christ" as we look down our noses at the "true Church of yesterday." The next time God moves and speaks, we had better be prepared to hear someone call themselves the "new true Church of Jesus Christ" as they look down their noses at us! (I think we have just discovered how denominations came into being.)

We Need One Another

God knows all things, and it is no accident that He has fixed things so that we have to connect with one another to accomplish His will. Historically, one group would move with God for a while (and build a monument to their revelation). No sooner would they settle into their new temple of revealed truth than God would begin to move again. But to follow Him forced the people to choose between their comfortable homestead of past revelation or the difficult road of new revelation and unknown challenges. Usually, only a remnant will come into the new revelation of God, while the majority remains behind to "fight against" the new revelation of God.

You should understand that when I say "new thing," I am aware that "there is nothing new under the sun" (Eccles. 1:9). However, this does not apply to the mercies and wonders of God, which no man can or ever will fully fathom. The fact is that when a different emphasis arises in the lives of obedient believers because of revelation, somehow the "new" group begins to become a threat to the "old" because they're saying and doing things that they didn't do before. That leads to the creation and application of "labels" to mark the "outsiders."

In the Book of Acts, believers were called "people of the way" at first. Then their opponents called them "Christians," a degrading term (in their minds) that means "little Christs" because they acted just like the renegade rabbi who had run around in Jerusalem, the rabbi they had called in the Greek, "Christ." They also tagged Christians with little names like "Ramonites," and accused them of belonging to a cult. They were the "people of another way, another persuasion...."

Beware of Pharisees

Again, this dislike of the new is a human trait. No one is automatically exempt from it. If we don't watch it, we will be get so busy expounding on what God is emphasizing that we will build tabernacles, walls, and structures around our new (and now "private") revelation. Then we will make it our responsibility to shoot rockets and drop negative "slander bombs" on anything that doesn't look like what we're doing.

This was the situation Paul ran into in Jerusalem. Some false brethren had infiltrated the home church to spy on their activities and liberties in Christ, hoping to gather evidence and forge a plan to bring them all back into bondage to the "Pharisaic way" of doing things (before Christ redeemed believers from the law on the cross). Paul was unmoved. He simply continued to do what God told him to do—he wrote, spoke, and ministered by revelation:

> *I do not frustrate the grace of God: for if righteousness come by the law, then Christ is dead in vain. O foolish Galatians, who hath bewitched you, that ye should not obey the truth, before whose eyes Jesus Christ hath been evidently set forth, crucified among you? This only would I learn of you, Received ye the Spirit by the works of the law, or by the hearing of faith? Are ye so foolish? having begun in the Spirit, are ye now made perfect by the flesh?* (Galatians 2:21–3:3)

God had exonerated the believers in Galatia, but misled men were trying to bring the believers there back into condemnation. God gave them freedom from bondage to be sons of God, and He brought them from defeat to victory. Now religious legalists were trying to say, "No, you're still defeated." Paul's revelation of the gospel of Christ delivered them from walking in the flesh, and they began to walk in the Spirit.

He was dealing with the difference between "walking in the flesh" and the fruit of the Spirit. Paul had delivered them from "falling from grace" to begin "walking and standing in grace." These are all battlegrounds that Paul addresses with the believers in Galatia:

*Tell me, ye that desire to be under the law, do ye not hear the law? For it is written, that Abraham had two sons, the one by a bondmaid, the other by a free-woman. But he who was of the bondwoman was born after the flesh; but he of the freewoman was **by promise**. Which things are an allegory: for these are the two covenants; the one from the mount Sinai, which gendereth to bondage, which is Agar. For this Agar is mount Sinai in Arabia, and answereth to Jerusalem which now is, and is in bondage with her children. But Jerusalem which is above is free, which is the mother of us all. For it is written, Rejoice, thou barren that bearest not; break forth and cry, thou that travailest not: **for the desolate hath many more children** than she which hath an husband* (Galatians 4:21-27).

How can a "desolate" or barren woman have more children than a woman who is not? All it takes is a word from God. Paul wrote, "Now we, brethren, as Isaac was, are the children of promise. But as then he that was born after the flesh persecuted him that was born after the Spirit, even so it is now" (Gal. 4:28-29).

"Wisdom" and the Spirit of Wisdom

That which is born after the flesh always tends to persecute that which is after the Spirit. People, things, and ideas that are birthed or rooted in the flesh will decay because they have nothing lasting in them. They are cut off from the continual flow of the Source of life. But those people, things, and ideas birthed in the Spirit of God will endure forever because they spring from the Source of all life and vitality—the Spirit of the Everlasting God. For this reason, even today we see that which is "born after the flesh" persecuting, hindering, and belittling that which is "born after the Spirit."

Persecution or opposition can be subtle sometimes. It may come to you in the form of little words spoken by trusted people who react to your growth in the Spirit by saying, "Well now, you had better use *wisdom* (as if it is *unwise* to grow in God). Tell me why Paul prayed "That the God of our Lord Jesus Christ, the Father of glory, may give unto you the *spirit of wisdom* and revelation in the knowledge of Him" (Eph. 1:17). Paul didn't run around telling people to "use wisdom." He prayed that God would give them a *spirit* of wisdom and of revelation!

"Well, I'm going to fast seven days."

"Better use wisdom. You know you have to go to work every day."

"What are you saying?"

"You'd better use wisdom."

"Well, when you fasted seven days, what did you do?"

"Oh, I used wisdom. I never fasted 7 days. I have enough wisdom to know better than not to eat for 7 days."

(The people who usually tell their friends to "use wisdom" in areas like fasting have never done anything for spiritual growth. They usually haven't ever fasted for a single day, or two days, let alone for 5, 10, or 40 days!)

You need to pray that God will give your friends and fellow believers a "spirit of wisdom and revelation of the knowledge of Him." If you know something through personal experience in the Lord, then share it! I've drawn from my fasting experiences to counsel friends contemplating a fast, "Just make sure you drink water. If you have a strenuous job, then maybe you need to take some liquid juice and mix it with water in the morning for some strength. If you're going to have a prolonged fast, then maybe you need to bathe more often because the impurities will begin to manifest themselves through your flesh." That is the sharing of wisdom, and the impartation of godly knowledge. The bottom line is that sometimes, "religious statements" can become distractions.

Innocent statements like, "You had better pray about that," are not given to exhort and edify, but to limit you! The unspoken motive behind the high-sounding words may be, *"I want to keep you where I am. Don't get too far ahead of me. Don't get out there."* Sarcastic or cynical statements from friends can weigh in heavily too. "You don't want to be a *fanatic* do you?" (A *fanatic* is simply "a fan.")

Even little statements or side comments can sometimes bring us into a yoke of bondage. I have been guilty of saying these kinds of things to people, and I have also experienced the correction of God. He had me go back and review my motives.

"Why did you say that to that person?"

"I was afraid that they might hurt themselves."

"Were you? Isn't that My child? Didn't I reveal Christ in them? Do you think I'm going to let them die on a fast to Me?"

"Well, God, what am I supposed to do?"

"Do what Paul did. Pray that I will give them a spirit of wisdom and revelation in the knowledge of Me."

Share What You Know

If you have wisdom, give it; but don't try to look spiritual and give hints that say, "I know something you don't know." If I know it, and I'm your brother or sister, then I will share it. That is what Paul did in his Epistle to the Colossians. First he described the revelation he was preaching to them, then he outlined the ways that he was imparting that wisdom to the people:

> *Whereof I am made a minister, according to the dispensation of God which is given to me for you, to fulfil the word of God; even the mystery which hath been hid from ages and from generations, but now is made manifest to His saints:* **to whom God would make known** *what is the riches of the glory of this mystery among the Gentiles; which is Christ in you, the hope of glory: whom we* **preach, warning** *every man, and teaching every man in all wisdom; that we may present every man perfect in Christ Jesus: whereunto I also labor, striving according to His working, which worketh in me mightily* (Colossians 1:25-29).

The same apostle who prayed that God would give believers a spirit of wisdom is saying he also *preached*, *warned*, and *taught* every man in wisdom. This apostle didn't just pray and then tell people to "go out and get God's wisdom." He also imparted, or shared, what he had. If you have it, then you need to give it. If you don't have it, then you need to pray that they get it. Otherwise, you will just create confusion by giving things "outside of spiritual wisdom."

We are still talking about moving from level to level in our walk with God. Notice what Paul told the Colossians: "Whereunto I also labour, striving according to His working, which worketh in me mightily. For I would that ye knew what great conflict I have for you..." (Col. 1:29–2:1). Paul said, "I labor, I am striving, I'm in conflict over you." The Greek word for "striving" is *agonitzome*, which means "to struggle, to compete for a prize, to contend with an adversary." He said, "I'm in a fight trying to get through this thing on your behalf."

Giants or Signs of Grace?

As I have said before, every time you get ready to break through into a greater revelation of God, you will face a fight and a struggle, you will face contention and striving. Not only will you be confronted by people who want to hold you down, but you will encounter spiritual forces that want to hinder and divert you from the purpose or plan of God for you in that level.

That is why the "giants" appeared when the Israelites entered their promised land. That is why I believe the Israelites looked at the walls of Jericho and said, "Man, I hope we can overtake it." You won't even see the giants until you step into your land of promise and destiny, but as soon as they show up, you will know you've landed at the door of a new level. When the fight begins, you will know you are getting ready to possess what God has promised you.

Many times the "big problems" you face are actually the outward or "manifest tokens" of the grace of God at work in your life as you endure. Paul told to the church at Thessalonica, "...we ourselves glory in you in the churches of God for your patience and faith in all your persecutions and tribulations that ye endure: which is a manifest token of the righteous judgment of God, that ye may be counted worthy of the kingdom of God, for which ye also suffer" (2 Thess. 1:4-5).

Sometimes the trials and afflictions come because you have caught hold of what God is saying. Troubles "reveal" those who are approved. People who dare to follow God stand out in a crowd where most people tend to shrink back from troubles or persecution for God's sake. The only way you can know what God said is for it to be revealed in you. You won't fight over what "somebody else" said. But once God speaks directly to you, the will to fight and stand the test will rise up in you! You'll say, "I saw it for myself. I *know* what God said, and it bore witness with my spirit. I saw it in the Book, and now there is a great conflict within me. I have to see it through."

Paul said he had a great conflict or struggle on behalf of the believers at Laodicea and everywhere else who had not personally seen his face. He longed to personally encourage them and increase their understanding of the mystery of God (Col. 2:1-2). He knew that our faith in Christ is always based on the word of revelation we personally receive in our hearts.

"So then faith cometh by hearing, and hearing by the word of God" (Rom. 10:17). God gave us His Word to accelerate and direct our upward progress, but you have to hear it over and over again. Faith comes when you hear God's Word. Once you hear His Word, you can stand steadfast knowing that God said it. I continually ask God before I take a stand in any issue or situation, "God, give me a word. Once You give me a word, I'll stand." I don't want to be standing on quicksand. I don't want to be standing in some man's wisdom and knowledge, but if God gives me a word, I'll stand on that.

Paul's Instruction for the Striving

For though I be absent in the flesh, yet am I with you in the spirit, joying and beholding your order, and the stedfastness of your faith in Christ. As ye have therefore received Christ Jesus the Lord, so walk ye in Him: rooted and built up in Him, and stablished in the faith, as ye have been taught, abounding therein with thanksgiving (Colossians 2:5-7).

Paul praised the believers at Colosse for their faith and stability, but then he gave them three solemn warnings that are vital to us today as we press in to the deeper things of God.

First, the apostle warned the Colossians, "Beware lest any man spoil you through philosophy and vain deceit, after the tradition of men, after the rudiments of the world, and not after Christ" (Col. 2:8). When something is spoiled, it is ruined. Paul warned that even someone who appeared to be running a "good race" could be "spoiled" by a little man-made philosophy, some vain deceit, or a dose of man's tradition and worldly patterns.

Paul is saying, "Beware! Don't let any man spoil you." The Greek term for "spoil" means "to lead as prey." In other words, you become "spoil" when someone puts a noose around your neck and makes you a victim rather than a victor.

How many "good people" have been "spoiled" by man's systems when they agreed to play the game of compromise to get promoted? "I don't care what you believe—just do it my way and I'll promote you. I'll take care of you. I'll even put you on staff one day." I would counsel people in that position to tell those folks, "No, you can just keep your promotion and job. I'd rather keep my integrity."

A lot of things are good, but they are "not God." They have to be spiritually discerned and examined, line upon line, precept upon precept, according to God's Word. When the Word of God is silent, then a man ought to be honest enough to say, "This is my preference, but it is not mandated by the Word of God."

Personal Preferences Are Permitted

We all do certain things according to preference, and not by divine command. There are things we "just don't have any verses for." Despite the unwillingness of many to admit it, the Bible does *not* say men should wear a suit and a tie to church services (nor does it forbid it). Most folks wore robes (or "A-line dresses" as we call them today) in the days of Christ, but that is not the way we dress today. Are we in sin? No! Frankly, God spells certain things out in His Word, He reserves some things for the leading of the Spirit, and He expects us to follow our preference our conscience in everything else.

Serious problems come when men falsely present their personal preferences as mandates from God's Word. This gives birth to the rudiments of men, and traditions of the flesh. It is deceitful to say, "We're doing this because it's in the Word," when it's not. You need to differentiate between the Word and the whim of man. You may prefer to have a multi-colored carpet on the floor, but you probably didn't do a lot of fasting and prayer about it. I dare you to show me a Bible verse that says, "Yea, I say unto you, thou shalt install gray carpet on thy floor—preferably with stain protection." No, you choose such things by preference, not through some deep, spiritual exercise.

I have vowed to God and myself that I will not walk in deceit. I tell it just the way it is. If something is a preference, then that is simply the way I prefer it to be. I don't try to tell people that I had a spiritual visitation or that some Bible verse told me I had to do it a certain way. In the Book of Acts you will see where an apostle or prophet might tell the people, "The Holy Ghost says...," and then at other times will say, "It seemed good to *us*...." There is a difference between a divine command and a human choice.

In cases where God permits us to choose by preference, He confirms our choices with His peace according to Colossians 3, which says: "And let the peace of God rule in your hearts, to the which also ye are called in one body; and be ye thankful" (Col. 3:15). Let the peace of God rule in your heart.

Paul offers a solution for dealing with those who try to spoil believers by substituting man-made solutions and "salvation by works" schemes for the gospel of Christ. He reaffirms the total and complete redemptive work of Christ at Calvary in the verses that follow, beginning with, "For in Him dwelleth all the fulness of the Godhead bodily. And ye are complete in Him, which is the head of all principality and power" (Col. 2:9-10).

Resist Judgment on the Individual

He vividly describes how Jesus Christ "spoiled the spoilers" when He "...spoiled principalities...[and] made a show of them openly, triumphing over them in it" (Col. 2:15). The apostle added a second warning to go with the first in verse 8:

> *Let no man therefore judge you in meat, or in drink, or in respect of an holyday, or of the new moon, or of the sabbath days: which are a shadow of things to come; but the body is of Christ* (Colossians 2:16-17).

Judgment can come our way in subtle ways and phrases. "Brother, you had better stay away from pork. And you know that wine is out." Judgment may be one of the most popular pastimes among church people today. Billy Graham once mentioned during a broadcast that he knew a lot of Christians all over the world who drink wine. He said his ministry received more negative mail over that comment than any other in the history of Billy Graham's ministry! All he said was, "I know Christians all over the world that drink wine. They're totally committed and sold out for Jesus Christ." Then he went on to add the statement that it was because the water is unfit to drink in many places in the world.

The second greatest volume of mail came in when he said, "There's as much gambling that goes on on Wall Street as happens in Las Vegas." He was right, but he was judged for it too.

Christians have a tendency to judge things too quickly. "That's wrong and this is right, and under no circumstances can those things be permitted or done." Yet Paul says, "Let no man therefore judge you in meat, or in drink, or in respect of an holyday..." (Col. 2:16). Some Christians celebrate Passover, Pentecost, and the Feast of Tabernacles, and some will not. Many American Christians celebrate Easter and Christmas, and some will not. The issue is this: We are not to judge each other over our personal choices.

If you want to put a Christmas tree with tinsel and lights in your house, then do it. If I don't do the same, then don't call me unspiritual because of my choice. Nor do I have the right to judge you because of what you do. Instead of obeying the direct command of God, we try to justify our prejudices and personal preferences. You will always find somebody trying to pull out some obscure Scriptures and saying, "Well, you know what Ezekiel said about bringing trees into your house...." My answer is: "Well, you know what Paul said about judging people over holy days...."

At every level of growth in your life, God will tell you personally to eliminate certain things in your life. You should just count on having someone come up to you to say, "Why, this is all right. What did you cut that out for?" You need to put all these things in the proper perspective.

We have a four-foot Christmas tree at our house that's been around since 1989. One year, about three months after Christmas, we got tired of looking at the thing, so we just threw a garbage bag over it and stored it in the basement. Every now and then on Christmas Eve, we pull that little tree out of the bag, light it up and let it burn for a little while. Then we put a garbage bag over it and put it back in the basement. I'm sure there are folks out there who would line up to "correct my error," but I refuse to be brought into bondage about a Christmas tree, the absence of a Christmas tree, or any other "non-issue."

When our kids opened their gifts, we never told them any wild stories about Santa Claus. I told them, "Look, your

Momma bought you this gift," or "Your Grandma brought this gift for you. Isn't it nice?" (That is, if we have gifts at all. Some years we just say, "We're not going to buy any gifts this year." One year we decided not to buy anything for our family. We all decided to buy gifts to give away to other people instead.

Don't let people judge you just because God has you walking a strict path to break tradition in your life. If you are one of those believers who says, "I can't come to church at Christmas time because we're getting our tree ready" or "I was at home cooking my turkey and roast. Besides, I had popcorn I had to string up for the tree," then don't be surprised if God says one day, "Cut that mess out." However, there may be other times when He will say, "Go ahead and enjoy it." The bottom line according to Paul is this: Don't let anybody judge you. And don't try to judge others either—you don't know what God is doing with them.

Paul also warned against judgment over "new moons" and Sabbath days. There are always those who come in say in an authoritative voice, "We ought to be worshiping on the Sabbath day—on Saturday, not Sunday." God says, "Break into the levels I've placed before you, and don't get tangled up in that other stuff."

The Bible refers to "that other stuff" as "shadows of things to come" (Col. 2:17a). What you need to do is find the "substance," which is the Body of Christ. Find the substance and leave the shadows alone. When I come home after a long ministry trip and my wife comes out to greet me out in the bright sunshine, I can see my wife. I can also see her shadow on the ground. Which one do you think I reach for? I guarantee you that I never fall on the ground and embrace that shadow. No sir, I look for the substance, not the shadow.

Real Humility, Rather Than Religious Externals

Paul's third warning was this: "Let no man beguile you of your reward in a voluntary humility and worshipping of angels, intruding into those things which he hath not seen, vainly puffed up by his fleshly mind" (Col. 2:18). He is saying, "Don't let anybody trick you out of your reward through false humility." Voluntary humility describes things or actions we might do to make people think we have some special level of piety or humility.

We often practice voluntary humility (or self-imposed humility) in the way that we make up our face (or *don't* make up our face). It may be in the way we dress ("Well, I never wear *those* kinds of clothes—I would never spend that kind of money on mere clothes"). Don't let anybody trick you into voluntary humility. Be humble, but let God work humility into you. I've seen people who are supposed to be "shamefaced." They take care to wear no makeup, no jewelry, and no "adornment," but sometimes the same people have more pride over their piety than anyone else! "I'm better than everybody else because I have my hair pulled back in a bun. I pulled my hair back so tight that it make me look Oriental because that's religious. I don't wear makeup or jewelry, and I'm proud because I'm righteous!" I'm sorry to break the news to you, but it is possible to do all these exterior things and become caught up in voluntary humility.

Paul warned about worshiping angels too. A man in Atlanta told me, "I'm ready to see an angel." I told him, "You don't want to see an angel, you want to see Christ." I explained that most of the folks in the Bible who had angels appear to them were either ignorant, lacking perception of the seasons of God, or in rebellion because they had failed to believe what God had said. Beguilers intrude into things they have not seen, and are "vainly puffed up by their fleshly minds" (Col. 2:18). If you don't walk in revelation, then you begin to imagine things just to be sensational. I believe in angels. I've heard a lot of testimonies about them, and I believe that I've even seen some myself. Yet I must move past that to get to Christ. Yes, I praise God for that experience, but *Christ is what I want*!

Paul warns us that the greatest danger of all this distraction from the "substance" of our faith is that we might find ourselves "...not holding the Head, from which all the body by joints and bands having nourishment ministered, and knit together, increaseth with the increase of God" (Col. 2:19).

Chapter 8

Perfected Through Struggle and Suffering

There are two great evidences of the genuine Christian life: your *faith* in the Lord and your *love* toward one another. Each of these shines brightest in the midst of difficulty and hardship, when faith and love are *not* the natural thing to expect from human beings. Paul the apostle emphasized these evidences in his joyous greeting to the Ephesian believers: "Wherefore I also, after I heard about your faith in the Lord Jesus, and love to all the saints" (Eph. 1:15).

Proof of His Presence

This faith is linked with the term *Lord Jesus* which speaks of what we *do* more than what we *say*. Jesus continues to ask, "And why call ye Me, Lord, Lord, and do not the things which I say?" (Lk. 6:46) When we see the word *Christ* it speaks of our position in the things of God and in the Spirit.

Paul reacted to these two proofs of Christ's presence among the Ephesians by saying:

[I] cease not to give thanks for you, making mention of you in my prayers; that the God of our Lord Jesus Christ, the Father of glory, may give unto you the spirit of wisdom and of revelation in the knowledge of Him (Ephesians 1:16-17).

A Continuous Revelation of God

The "spirit of revelation" unfolds or unveils God's truth unto us. Paul prayed for the Ephesians so that "the eye of their understanding would be enlightened" so they could understand what the Spirit of God was doing and saying. Everything God does calls and compels us into more of Him. He takes us from level to level of maturity so we can obtain a greater revelation and unveiling of the knowledge of Him—not to help us accumulate "more knowledge" so that we can "get deep."

As the knowledge of God is unveiled more and more in us, there should also be a greater manifestation of Him inside of us. Paul said God has "...put all things under His [Jesus'] feet, and gave Him to be the head over all things to the church, which is His body, the fulness of Him that filleth all in all" (Eph. 1:22-23). What is the Church? It is His body, the fulness of Him that filleth all in all. We grow up into Him and advance into new levels of maturity in Him. It will always involve a deeper understanding, revelation, and unveiling of Him.

In his Epistle to the Galatians, Paul said:

But when it pleased God, who separated me from my mother's womb, and called me by His grace, to reveal His Son in me, that I might preach Him among the heathen; immediately I conferred not with flesh and blood (Galatians 1:15-16).

Where does Paul say that God revealed His Son? Did you notice that he did *not* say Jesus was revealed "unto me," but "in me"? Day by day there should be an uncovering and unfolding of God's Son *in you.*

That also confirms that growth doesn't come with mere head knowledge or the accumulation of facts. Growth occurs as God's Son is revealed and manifested in us. This revelation is a work of illumination, inspiration, and ultimately, transformation. Paul said God's grace revealed His Son in him that he "might preach Him among the heathen." Then he says something that we've mentioned before: "Immediately I conferred not with flesh and blood, neither went I to Jerusalem to them that were apostles before me; but I went into Arabia and returned again unto Damascus" (Gal. 1:16b-17).

When God reveals something to you, don't rush out to tell everybody about it. Spend some time alone with God and allow the Holy Spirit to hover over the revelation so that He can reveal it more clearly to you. Then you can speak about it, even if you haven't walked in it yet. God wants to reveal Himself *in you*, and there are some things that can only be received and shared by revelation (such as Peter's revelation that Jesus was the Son of God in Matthew 16:17).

Some people have been caught up to Heaven where they saw all kinds of glory, but this is the experience of only a few. The only way most of us can talk about Heaven is by revelation. The same is true of hell (if you were placed in hell, you would still be there). There are a lot of things that you have not experienced, but God will reveal them in you.

Think about this for a moment: The same Almighty God who cannot be contained in walls or in temples has chosen to dwell *in you*, where He continually unveils and reveals Himself directly to our inner man. When that revelation is imparted, His Spirit hovers over the revelation until it "comes forth or manifests itself *in us*.

The last Book of the Bible is called the Revelation of the Lord Jesus Christ. The whole book deals with the revelation of Jesus Christ. John begins in Revelation 1:10 by saying, "I was in the spirit on the Lord's day...." Throughout the book, John must use spiritual language to describe "what was, what is, and what is to come," which could only be received by revelation. It is clear in this book and elsewhere in His Word that God wants to show us what kind of travail and suffering must take place to bring forth the glory of God in the earth.

Revelation Manifested Through Labor

People who fail to understand that the Book of Revelation is exactly that—a revelation and manifestation of the tribulation, pain, and spiritual birth process needed for God to bring forth His heavenly Kingdom in the earth—feel the need to close the book and do all kinds of weird "literal" stuff with those spiritual images and truths, like concocting "locust helicopters" and the like. "Well, John's talking about natural stuff, LaFayette." If you believe that, then what do you do with the harlot woman who's sitting on seven mountains? If it's literal, then either we're dealing with a pretty big sister or some awfully small mountains!

When you get in the Spirit as John was when he received the revelation, you can understand what's going on (by revelation). Babylon has always been a symbol of false religions. Mountains are often symbolic of countries, nations, rules or domains, and regions.

John said, "I was *in the spirit* on the Lord's day." The natural mind cannot discern the things of the Spirit. When a man tells you that he was in the Spirit, then you have to spiritually discern the things that were, that are, and that are to come. If you will approach the Book of Revelation with the understanding that it is actually a *revelation*, and ask yourself, "What will it take for earth to bring forth Jesus?" then this book will open up to you. It will begin to make sense to you. Above all, we shouldn't be afraid of this book because of its "end times" nature. The Word says, "Blessed is he that readeth, and they that hear the words of this prophecy" (Rev. 1:3a). Our response should be, "God, open my eyes. Give me the spirit of wisdom and revelation."

The Baby's Coming...

No revelation comes without great stress, pressure, and pain. Every time God gets ready to reveal more of Himself within you, it's just like undergoing another birth. Your natural birth came forth with pain. First, your mother became impregnated when the egg within her was fertilized with seed. Then after gestation and preparation, there was pain. The final birth process starts off with just a few tremors and a little bit of swelling and contraction. Then the birth begins in earnest, and the pain of bringing forth the new life begins. The closer a woman gets to the actual birth, the sharper her pain becomes.

At the very last moment, when she wants to withdraw, when she is ready to throw out all the doctors and nurses, just before she grabs her husband by the throat to choke him and forcefully tell him, "Don't you ever touch me or come near me again," she hears the doctor say, "It's time for you to push."

Invariably, this comes at the time of greatest pain. This is when the doctor says, "Push!" He doesn't say, "Quit," or "Get weary in well doing." No, at the time of the greatest pain, when the pressure is the most severe, when it looks like all you want to say is, "I quit," that is when he says, "Bear down and push that thing forth." You may be in a lot of pain right now, but it's not time for drawing back. If you listen closely, you will hear the Spirit say: "Bear down, focus, and push that thing on through!"

The apostle Paul almost presents the picture of a woman laboring to bring forth a child into the world as he wrote to the Philippians; only he was speaking by the Spirit when he said "...this one thing I do, forgetting those things which are behind, and reaching forth unto those things which are before, I press toward the mark for the prize of the high calling of God in Christ Jesus" (Phil. 3:13-14).

The writer of Hebrews said, "But we are not of them who draw back unto perdition; but of them that believe to the saving of the soul" (Heb. 10:39). God is telling us to bear down and push that thing through. God wants you to push the most at the height and time of your greatest pain. When your situation and circumstances don't look right, God says, "It's you time to bring forth. Don't abort this new thing I have planted within you—don't let it go."

I've discovered in the moments of my greatest pain and stress that even as God says, "Push, LaFayette," suddenly people will begin to come up to me and say, "I'm praying for you. I just want you to know—I'm praying for you." They didn't know what I was going through, but God's Word says that Jesus is our high priest who "ever liveth to make intercession" for us (see Heb. 7:25). I've learned that He speaks to the hearts of His saints supernaturally and says, "Pray for the pastor. Pray for your sister. Pray for your brother." God will make a way if you will agree to stay. Decide you will not abort what God has placed within you, and submit to the process.

There is no birthing without painful, stretching labor. The spiritual "work" of intercession involves pain and a sort of "death." When we work and struggle in Spirit-led prayer and intercession, the Spirit helps us remove the old things in our lives and in the lives of those we pray for, so that the new things and revelations of God can be brought forth.

The "baby" you are carrying in your spiritual "womb" is real—it is just invisible. That is where faith comes in. Hebrews 11 declares, "Now faith is the substance of things hoped for, the evidence of things not seen" (Heb. 11:1). When a woman goes to a doctor for prenatal care, she knows the doctor has various devices and techniques to perceive and examine the baby she knows is there, but which the world doesn't see. God says, "I want the world to see the baby in you." Therefore, in nine months, this new life must come forth. When the timing of the Lord comes, He says, "It is time. This holy seed must be born! You can't stay pregnant all the time."

We are bound to thank God always for you, brethren, as it is meet, because that your faith groweth exceedingly, and the charity of every one of you all toward each other aboundeth, so that we ourselves glory in the churches of God for your patience and faith in all your persecutions and tribulations that you endure (2 Thessalonians 1:3-4).

Paul said, "...we ourselves glory" in you. One of the things God wants to do is to reveal His Son in us and at the same time reveal His glory in us. No, that doesn't mean we can "touch the glory" that belongs solely to Him and get any credit for it. Yet there is this glorious *doxa*, this glory, the character of the Renown, the weight of God. He wants to reveal that thing in us! Paul directly relates the revelation of God's *doxa* (glory) in the Church with the struggle and suffering of the saints. This is the "manifest token of the righteous judgment of God..." (2 Thess. 1:5). What is Paul talking about? If these persecutions and tribulations that we're enduring are a "manifest token of the righteous judgment of God," then why would God judge us like this? Paul finishes verse five of Second Thessalonians 1 with the words, "...that you may be counted worthy of the kingdom of God...."

Birth Is Just the Beginning

It is one thing to be born again, but Jesus said, "Except a man be born again, he cannot *see the kingdom of God*" (Jn. 3:3b). Then He went a step further and said, "...Except a man be born of...the Spirit, he cannot *enter* into the kingdom of God" (Jn. 3:5). In the Book of Acts, Paul told some disciples during a missionary journey. "We must *through much tribulation* enter into the kingdom of God" (Acts 14:22). Some people have been born again but have never entered into the Kingdom of God because every time there was resistance and pressure, they stopped.

I you want to grow and move up into new levels, then expect to go through some tribulation and suffering. Suffering is not a bad word. It speaks of the experience, sensation, or impression of being in pain for the Kingdom of God.

Paul wrote, "...it is a righteous thing with God to recompense tribulation to them that trouble you" (2 Thess. 1:6). Suffering and persecution often come at the hands of people, but no one can touch God's anointed without great risk. There are those who will come into your life to trouble you, but your suffering in these trials and troubles will make you worthy of the Kingdom of God.

God Will Take Care of You

Jesus warned us that our enemies may even be those of your own household (Lk. 12:51-53). I don't know about you, but I want my house to be a place of peace. If this is your desire, then as you labor and travail in prayer, you will see everyone come in and enter the Kingdom; and your home will come to peace in the end. Yet you will have seasons of "trouble" marked by seemingly continuous labor, travail, and suffering.

To everyone experiencing a season of "trouble," Paul says, "And to you who are troubled rest with us" (2 Thess. 1:7a). The apostle is issuing an invitation to "relax, experience relief, and cease from your labor." When you are troubled, resist the temptation to get in the flesh and fight back. When someone speaks slanderously about you, don't make arrangements to get their car towed! If someone assaults you physically or verbally, don't "assault them back." If someone reviles you without cause, don't set out to "revile them back." The Bible says, "Just rest." Why? The key is found in the previous verse. God is righteous, and He is more than able and willing to take care of you while "rewarding" your persecutors and false accusers. Go through your tribulation with hope, and learn the lesson thoroughly. Get everything God wants for you in that circumstance.

God's Plan for the Persecutor

Ancient Israel used to mess up grandly. They ran off to worship other gods, sacrificed their children to demons, and did all kinds of crazy stuff. Then God would send in Syria or some other nearby nation to bring Israel to her knees because He knew that the only way the Jews would turn back was through tribulation. Out of their pain, the Israelites would cry unto the Lord, and He would bring them out of captivity. Then God would say, "Now Syria, you messed up because you hurt My people! Now I'm going to turn My attention to you." Then He would slay them for not following His instructions. "I told you to bring them into captivity, but I didn't tell you to kill them."

When Israel messed up again, God would say, "Babylon, you will be My hand, My rod of correction. Chase Israel." When the Babylonians were too hard on Israel, then God would hear their cries of distress and say, "Okay, I'm going to raise up the Meads and Persians to deliver you from Babylon and punish your persecutors." The Old Testament was given as an example to us. Every person God used as a rod of punishment was later on punished. We've seen that in the Body of Christ in recent years. Every Christian leader who has risen up to publicly pronounce judgment on another brother has been "recompensed" the same thing. God is warning us not to be severe with our brothers.

Although outward ceremonial laws change, God's moral laws and standards of right and wrong do not change. The New Testament truth of forgiveness, mercy, and grace through Christ appears to be different from the harsher system based on "an eye for an eye and a tooth for a tooth" in the Old Testament. Yet the truth is that salvation by faith through Christ is a return to the relationship-based existence we see first in the garden of Eden. It was sin that created the deviation to "life under the law" in the Old Covenant.

Paul devoted three verses to a description of the fiery vengeance God bring to our ungodly persecutors (see 2 Thess. 1:7-9). God will judge. When it's time for God to be glorified in you, He will put down all persecution and tribulation that has resisted that process. We are tasting of that righteous judgment today, and we will see its full culmination in the days to come.

God's Plan for the Predestined

I believe in eternal judgment. I believe the appointed day will come when God will judge everything with "everlasting destruction from the presence of the Lord," so that His glory can be revealed in those that admire Him (2 Thess. 1:9-10). Paul describes the final goal of this process in verse 11:

Wherefore also we pray always for you, that our God would count you worthy of this calling, and fulfil all the good pleasure of His goodness, and the work of faith with power: that the name of our Lord Jesus Christ may be glorified in you, and ye in Him, according to the grace of our God and the Lord Jesus Christ (2 Thessalonians 1:11-12).

It is God's plan for the name of Jesus to be glorified *in you*! Paul further describes this process in the Book of Romans:

For whom He did foreknow, He also did predestinate to be conformed to the image of His Son, that He might be the firstborn among many brethren. Moreover whom He did predestinate, them He also called; and whom He called, them He also justified; and whom He justified, them He also glorified (Romans 8:29-30).

God wants you to understand that your destiny (and the key to your growth) is for Christ to be revealed in you so He can glorify you. He has predestined you to be conformed unto the image of His dear Son.

Chapter 9

Bearing the Load
in Times of Trouble

Blessed be God, even the Father of our Lord Jesus Christ, the Father of mercies and the God of all comfort; who comforteth us in all our tribulation, that we may be able to comfort them which are also in trouble... (2 Corinthians 1:3-4).

Trouble is the middle name" of growth and progress in the Christian life. It is often the valley of the shadow of death between mountain "A" and mountain "B." God proves us through the times of trouble, tribulation, persecution, and testing that come our way. Does this mean that He really "wonders" where you are in spiritual things? No, He already knows where you are, but He uses adversity to perfect you, and to reveal to *you* where you are and what He is doing in your life.

Speaking From Experience...

Paul says God comforts us "in all our tribulation, *that we may be able to comfort them which are in any trouble*" (2 Cor.

1:4a). If you haven't gone through hardship or desperate pain of some kind, then you will find it difficult or impossible to *effectively* comfort people who are going through suffering and tribulation. (I emphasized "effective" because anyone can offer hurting people help in the form of trite sayings, thoughtless sentiments, and flowers or cards. These things are powerless to comfort the hurting!)

On the other hand, once you have gone through the fire of adversity and tribulation and personally experienced God's comfort in the midst of your mess, you will be different. I guarantee you will have a different kind of compassion and understanding for other hurting people. You will have a special sensitivity to people who are experiencing painful trials and difficulties.

The Consolation of Endurance

For as the sufferings of Christ abound in us, so our consolation [which is the ministry of comfort] *also aboundeth by Christ. And whether we be afflicted, it is for your consolation and salvation, which is effectual in the enduring in the same sufferings which we also suffer* (2 Corinthians 1:5-6).

The Greek word translated "endure" is *hupomeno*. It means "to come up under, or remain." It literally means "to sustain a load." God is calling us in the midst of our trouble, persecution, and tribulation, to bear up under the load. This is contrary to our natural tendency to quit when we go through tribulation, persecution, and trouble. I've got some news for you: God is out to pull all the "quit" out of you! He says, "Take My yoke upon you, and learn of Me; for I am meek and lowly in heart: and ye shall find rest unto your souls. For My yoke is easy, and My burden is light" (Mt. 11:29-30).

Right in the midst of our troubles, tribulations, and persecution, God imparts to us a consolation called "endurance." The Greek root of this word is the same word from which we get *parakletos*, "the comforter, to comfort, the intercessor." This consolation comes alongside to strengthen you so that you can bear up under the load—no matter what load is placed upon you.

Paul also says, "And our hope of you is stedfast, knowing, that as ye are partakers of the sufferings, so shall ye be also of the consolation" (2 Cor. 1:7). If we want to understand the consolation of God, we must then be partakers of His suffering. If we want to move on to higher levels in Christ, we must expect times of proving and testing. Paul, the author of a majority of the books of the New Testament, offers his own life experience as an example:

> *For we would not, brethren, have you ignorant of our trouble which came to us in Asia, that we were pressed out of measure, above strength, insomuch that we despaired even of life: but we had the sentence of death in ourselves, that we should not trust in ourselves, but in God which raiseth the dead: who delivered us from so great a death, and doth deliver: in whom we trust that He will yet deliver us* (2 Corinthians 1:8-10).

Deliverance in Death

Paul saw trouble as something that "comes after" us. He knew we wouldn't choose it or willing set aside times for "suffering." Nobody prays, "God prove me. Send trouble, tribulation, persecution my way so I can know who I really am."

One day I did ask God to "show me who I was." I was having a stretch of several good days back to back, and I felt real spiritual. God began to show me my pride and my lustful thoughts. He uncovered my hidden motives and reminded me of certain "righteous" actions and said, "You just did that to be seen." Once God showed me who I was, my prayer changed. I began to pray, "God don't show me anymore. Just give me some grace. Show me the blood. Show me Your mercy."

Paul told the Corinthians, "We were pressed out of measure, above strength, insomuch that we despaired even of life" (2 Cor. 1:8b). That is a pretty strong brand of trouble. Right in the middle of your trouble, you might feel like crying out, "God, this is killing me!" (I believe I can hear the Holy Spirit say, "Yeah, I know.") This may sound odd, but at times God is more interested in our death than in our life! We must die to ourselves so that the life of Christ may be produced in us. Remember: there can be no resurrected life unless we know Him in His death.

Paul said he wanted to be "found in Christ" that he might "...know Him, and the power of His resurrection, and the fellowship of His sufferings, being made conformable unto His death; if by any means I might attain unto the resurrection of the dead" (Phil. 3:10-11). Do you want to be conformed unto the Lord Jesus Christ? The only way this can happen is through death to self. At every level, there will be a working of death in your life. There can be no resurrected life without a death, and there can be no death without suffering.

Paul said, "But we had the sentence of death in ourselves, that we should not trust in ourselves, but in God which raiseth the dead" (2 Cor. 1:9). At each new level, God wants to bring us through death to the place where we understand that we cannot trust in anything else except Him. Before He says, "Go ye," in a new level, He first says "Come unto Me." Then He says, "...If any man will come after Me, let him deny himself, and take up his cross daily, and follow Me" (Lk. 9:23).

Every time God has given me a vision to go somewhere or do something, He first drew me unto Him. I can see a certain death at work in my life through suffering, trouble, and persecution. Yet at the same time, I am consoled with the Comforter and with His consolation that strengthens me and gives me endurance. In the midst of my trouble, persecution, and suffering, I can say, "Thanks be to God who always causes me to triumph in His love." If I get my eye set on the joy that is being set before me, I can endure my cross today with joy. The only way you can endure a fiery trial is to understand the end result of that trial.

The Process of Deliverance

God has three phases of deliverance from trouble, persecution, and death. He *has delivered*, He *does deliver,* and He *will yet deliver.* God hasn't brought you out of bondage just to end your life. You were saved for a reason. He brought you through the wilderness to bring you into the land of promise. Sometimes people come to my office and explain the trials, persecutions, and sufferings that they are experiencing. Sometimes God lets me pray with them in the midst of that—just to let them know that God *is* a deliverer. But there are also times when God says, "You better go ahead and tell them that once they get through this, *the whole process will start all over again."* So I tell them, "I want you to understand that the same God who *brought* you through and who *is bringing* you through *will be there to bring you* through in the days to come."

> *So also Christ glorified not Himself to be made an high priest; but He that said unto Him, Thou art My Son, to day have I begotten Thee. As He saith also in another place, Thou art a priest for ever after the order of Melchisedec. Who in the days of His flesh, when He had offered up prayers and supplications with strong crying and tears unto Him that was able to save Him from death, and was heard in that He feared; though He were a Son, yet learned He obedience by the things which He suffered* (Hebrews 5:5-8).

Why? "And being made perfect, He became the author of eternal salvation unto all them that obey Him" (Heb. 5:9). Christ was made perfect. He learned obedience by the things He suffered, but then He was made perfect through that same process and became a high priest unto an eternal salvation. Why? He learned obedience through the things that He suffered.

Peter warned, "Beloved, think it not strange concerning the fiery trial which is to try you, as though some strange thing happened unto you" (1 Pet. 4:12). Remember that fiery trials come to perfect the things God has placed within you. He wants you to build upon foundations of silver (your salvation), gold (which is the very character of Christ), and precious stones (symbolizing the Body of Christ). Unlike foundations of perishable wood, hay, and stubble, that will burn up in a fire like chaff, these precious materials will survive the hottest of times. Above all, don't think that you are exempt from fiery trials. Don't pray "Woe is me" and "Why me?" prayers. Why not you? It's your turn. Your time will come to be proven and perfected through trial by fire.

Purged and Perfected

...He that cometh after me is mightier than I, whose shoes I am not worthy to bear: He shall baptize you with the Holy Ghost, and with fire: whose fan is in His hand, and He will throughly purge His floor, and gather His wheat into the garner; but He will burn up the chaff with unquenchable fire (Matthew 3:11-12).

Jesus is purging the place where you are standing. He's about to send fire right down to the root of your being and character. He is saying, "You have experienced the baptism of the Holy Ghost for witnessing, power, and demonstration. Yet you and those around you ask, 'Why don't we see the miracles that our forefathers saw?' You need to go back and get the fire! If I gave you a miracle right now, I would be giving license to laziness."

Some of us won't even pray, and we refuse to fast (it's "too hard on the body"). Many of us have to fight and struggle just to go to church. For these reasons, God says, "If I give license to laziness, I will also be giving consent to some of your actions and appetites that need to be purged out. If I would bless you with all of these things attached, you'd be dangerous. You would be of no benefit to My Body, the Church." Therefore, I can only give you some limited signs every now and then, but not at the level of consistency your fathers saw. These are confirming signs that you are on the right road. And behind every sign, wonder, and miracle, I will send fire to purge that next level before you. In every place your feet will stand, you must meet a burning bush."

In each new place God will say, "The place where you are standing is holy ground. Take off your shoes, walk in Me now." Time and again, you will have a "burning bush" experience in which you encounter the fire that descends from Heaven. In every place you go, a fiery trial will be waiting to try you. Don't think it strange when you fall into any of these things. Simply understand that this is "part of the package" and one of the benefits you received when you were saved. You are destined for perfection; and even though you don't pray for or look for the process, as you break into new levels of maturity and power there will be times of proving and testing by way of fiery trial.

As usual, most of us "forget" Peter's warning and *think it's strange*. "Why me?" we whine. "Look at all these other saints! Why aren't they being assaulted? Why does God choose me? I'm trying to live right and do right. I'm singing in the choir, going to church every day, and reading my Bible. And then there's Sister Carnal. She gets away with everything. She calls everybody up on the phone and gossips. She creates constant mischief among the brethren. Why doesn't she have any problems?"

God is saying, "I'm proving you. I'm bringing you forth. The only way you will be brought forth is through the fire. I permitted the fiery trials to come your way, so don't think it strange."

But rejoice, inasmuch as ye are partakers of Christ's sufferings; that, when His glory shall be revealed, ye may be glad also with exceeding joy. If ye be reproached for the name of Christ, happy are ye; for the Spirit of glory and of God resteth upon you (1 Peter 4:13-14a).

Don't sit around thinking how strange it is that you've found yourself in a fire—rejoice! Get full of joy and shout joyfully unto God, "My God, I rejoice in You; not for the thing, but in the midst of it. Because I see the glory that has been set before me, in the very midst of this mess, I rejoice in You!" (Sometimes the "man on the inside" knows more about what you should be doing than your mind does.) At times, you will just have to command your stubborn soul, "Bless the Lord, oh, my soul!" Your spirit is always rejoicing, but you have to command your soul. "My soul doeth magnify the Lord. My spirit has to rejoice in Christ my Savior."

Strength Through Thanksgiving

There are some things I do because I've been commanded to do them, not because I *feel* like doing them. "To obey is better than sacrifice" according to First Samuel 15:22. I like to put obedience and sacrifice together and bring the sacrifice of praise into the house of the Lord. So even though I don't feel like it after I've been assaulted, sometimes I lift my hands and say, "Father, I thank You for this wrongful assault. I know You are proving me and causing me to be steadfast in the midst of this. Cause me not to be taken over to the will of my enemies. Help me to stand fast and sanctify this ground upon which I stand. You said that the ground on which I stand is holy ground, and I am standing on this ground, God. Don't let me be moved. Don't let me be shaken. I rejoice in You because You are my strength."

I have also discovered that the joy of the Lord is my strength! There is strength that comes every time you stand in the middle of the trouble and rejoice. You come away being strengthened because you rejoiced in the Lord, for God inhabits the praises of His people (Ps. 22:3). One of the ways we praise God is by rejoicing in Him. It is ironic that one of the things that causes God to rejoice is seeing His kids standing strong. He said of Job, "Have you considered My servant Job? There is none like him" (paraphrased from Job 1:8). That blesses God.

God watched Job stand and continue to praise Him through seemingly endless calamity and suffering. Although he lost everything but his life, this man held fast to his testimony and refused to let go of his integrity. Finally God said, "Enough!" and He threw that hedge of protection back up around the man. Then God said, "Because you were assaulted and yet did well, you get a bonus, Job. Not only do you get back everything the devil stole from you, but I will multiply it back to you. I rejoice when you are strong" (see Job 42).

It's when we are weak that we are strong. God's Word says He resists the proud, but He gives grace to the humble (1 Pet. 5:5b). That's the conditional grace God gives you. You've heard about unconditional grace, but there is also a conditional grace that God sets aside for the humble. He delights in covering and lifting up the humble man or woman, who admits, "I can't stand by myself. I need You to stand up big in Me."

Pressing Ahead Under Pressure

Sometimes I have to pray, "God, You stand up big in me because I feel like sitting down. I feel like backing up." All progress stops the minute we withdraw. Many times the agony and pressure of a trial is so strong that we want to withdraw from the conflict. Yes, the agony does stop or decrease when we withdraw, but so does progress. God says, "Now the just shall live by faith: but if any man draw back, My soul shall have no pleasure in him" (Heb. 10:38). So we must also say with the writer of the Book of Hebrews, "But we are not of them who draw back unto perdition; but of them that believe to the saving of the soul" (Heb. 10:39).

We are not drawing back, we are pressing ahead to the full assurance of our faith. God has called you and I to be trees of righteousness that are planted in the house of the Lord. We will flourish in the courts of our God. He has called you to be a tree planted by the rivers of water where your roots go deep and absorb the life-giving moisture of the ground. In the times of storm and drought, when everything else around you is withering, withdrawing, and dropping to the ground in defeat, your leaf will not whither (even though you may feel like quitting).

You will survive and flourish because in the times of the dew and in the wet season, you let your roots sink down. In the season of God, He says to you, "It is time for you to eat. It is time for you to pray. The soil is soft, and you can sink your roots deeply in Me. You may feel like you are failing and falling, and your thirst and fatigue may seem overpowering. But if you'll go down deep enough and tap into the ground waters of My abundance, then when your time comes to shoot up—even in the times of drought when everything else is withering away—you will stand and flourish because you are rooted deeply in My river of life. Remember: *Everything goes down before it goes up."*

A Sanctified Sacrifice

God sanctifies us "from the foot up." When you go into the Holy of Holies, remember that sanctification starts at the foot of the cross. The tabernacle of Moses was set up like a cross in a perfect Old Covenant picture of the New Covenant reality. At the foot of the tabernacle's cross (again the pattern comes to light), the Old Covenant priest first encountered the brazen altar in the outer court. This was the place of burning, the altar of sacrifice, the place of fire. As a New Covenant priest, God says to you as you stand before the place of burning and sacrifice, "I'm going to come down to the root of your character and motivation. In My love, I will strike a fire that will sanctify and bless everything from the foot to the crown."

After the fiery trials burn away chaff, the washing of the Word of God and the Spirit at the "laver," just beyond the altar, brings cleansing. Next you enter the inner court, where the two pieces of the cross intersect. It is here that you offer the shewbread, light the olive oil lamp of God, and offer sweet incense to the Most Holy God. This speaks of the oil of anointing, which always runs down. The Psalmist writing of unity said, "It is like the precious ointment [of anointing] upon the head, that ran down upon the beard, even Aaron's beard: that went down to the skirts of his garments" (Ps. 133:2).

Sanctification runs upward, as a flame that starts at the core of your being and rises up inside of you. When this purifying fire rises and the holy anointing descends to bring both elements together, you become a sweet-smelling savor unto God! The anointing coming down and the fire rising up touch and release a sweet aroma and blessed fragrance in the nostrils of God and man. This inward work corresponds to the Old Covenant priestly functions that took place in the Holy Place, the middle court reserved for the priests who offered sweet incense and anointing oil to God. God says, "Anoint the table of shewbread, anoint the golden candlestick, anoint the altar of incense. Take the elements of incense and join them with the flames of the fire on the golden altar of incense. Let them come together that I may receive a sweet fragrance from your innermost being—the fragrance of rejoicing."

Rejoicing in Adversity

"But rejoice, inasmuch as ye are partakers of Christ's sufferings; that, when His glory shall be revealed, ye may be glad also with exceeding joy" (1 Pet. 4:13). If I look at the sufferings of Christ and see the great benefit Christ received through it, then I can rejoice. Why? If I am partaking or sharing in the suffering of Christ, then according to Peter, I will receive the same benefit! I will be called a son of God through the things that I suffered in obedience.

Rejoicing and joy take on different qualities and intensity according to your position on "the cross" at any given time. In the midst of the fires of adversity and trial, you offer a sacrifice of praise, rejoicing in tears over the thing you are hoping for, the "joy set before you." At the altar of sacrifice and fire, you rejoice in faith, for faith is the "substance of things hoped for, the evidence of things not seen" (Heb. 11:1). Then there is the "exceeding great joy" in the Holy of Holies, when in the presence of God, the fruit of your faith becomes manifest. When that for which you have longed and sacrificed emerges from the hope realm into the reality, you will experience exceeding great joy!

Job "rejoiced" in faith despite the rejection he felt the day his friends put their elbows on his bed of affliction and said, "We know you must have committed a secret sin." When his mate said, "Why don't you just curse God and die?" he still rejoiced in His God and held onto his integrity (that was all he had left). Finally, Job even began to question things himself, saying, "Why is God permitting these things to happen?" Then he repented in his own heart and began to pray for these who had come and accused him. Then God sent another comforter to comfort him. Job began to rejoice, and God turned his captivity. Job reached the place where he said, "Lord, even though You slay me, yet I will serve You" (see Job 13:15). At that point an exceeding great joy began to come from his lips.

"If ye be reproached for the name of Christ, happy are ye; for the spirit of glory and of God resteth upon you: on their part He is evil spoken of, but on your part He is glorified" (1 Pet. 4:14). When you experience reproach, you may want to say, "I want to see His glory." Do you know how you get the spirit of glory? That spirit rests upon you when you suffer reproach for Christ.

"Well what about all that satanic stuff, like sickness and disease? Should I just welcome that stuff into my life?" No! Most of us have already been taught enough about what is satanic and what comes about through God's hand. This message on godly suffering is just the other side of that message.

Trial Before Triumph

Sometimes we hear so much positional truth about our healing, our anointing, our identity in Christ, and our fellowship in the secret place of the Most High, that we may begin to think we are "exempt" from adversity. If that is the case, then why does God call us victors? You cannot become a victor unless you have gone through some battles and won a victory!

If you are trying to "bear the load" in times of trouble, just make sure the "trouble" isn't of your own making. Peter warned us, "But let none of you suffer as a murderer, or as a thief, or as an evildoer, or as a busybody in other men's matters" (1 Pet. 4:15). If you are going to suffer, let it be the suffering of Christ. Don't commit a crime or cheat on your income taxes and say, "I'm being persecuted by the police. Or the IRS is out to get me." Don't do evil things. Don't show off. Don't show up late to work, and don't behave inappropriately at your job and steal the company's time. If you are called in for disciplinary actions because of these things, don't call those measures "persecution." It is simply justice. You will simply be reaping the reward and consequences of your own bad decisions. Yet the spirit of glory will rest upon you if you suffer for Christ and in Christ.

None of us are exempt from trouble. Anyone who has lived a Christian life for long understands that basically everyone gets hit and assaulted by the same things. You may ask, "Why does it seem like some people never get hit with anything?" It's not that they don't get hit, they just know how to respond.

I tell people who are in the middle of a great trial, "I want you to maintain high visibility." I explain to them that I don't want them to drift out of the doors the church building, "slip out" of services before the invitation is given, or avoid all contact with other believers. God tends to help His people "in the midst of the tabernacle." I know that we are the "habitation" of God, but He especially meets us in His corporate dwelling where the many temples of God meet together as one and release a mighty river of His anointing and manifest presence.

It's a Family Matter

When you are hurting or feeling the heat of the flames more than usual, run home to your spiritual family. Bask in the healing waters of the river of life that flows from New Jerusalem, the Church. The river of God runs between banks lined with the trees of the Lord, that are for the healing for the nations. It flows in the midst of God's prized heritage, you and me. Do you feel weary and heavy laden? Come on in and take the plunge.

The Scriptures declare that rivers of living water spring up from deep within the followers of Jesus Christ (Jn. 4:13-14). As we gather together, we join our individual tributaries of glory into one great flood of God's manifest glory as we join our voices into one voice of praise and worship to the Most High God. If you come in depressed, you can jump in and God will break totally snap that yoke of depression. No matter how weak you may feel, there is healing in the presence of God.

Feel the Flow of God's Life

Bring your stream of living water to flow (however weakly or uncertainly) into the midst of the living tabernacles of the Most High in the house of the Lord. Discover the crystal clear river that runs up and down among your brethren. The very moment you don't feel like being there is the very moment you most urgently *need* to be there! When your flesh and your soul resist your need for fellowship with the brethren in Christ, that's the time to boldly say, "I've gotta go swimming!" Take the plunge into Jesus Christ. Immerse yourself over your head in the steam of living water, the Spirit of God, for refreshing, for cleansing, and for new life. This river is deep enough to swim in, and it is well able to hold you up. Make no mistake about it: It is God who put in waters deep enough to either drown you or to effortlessly hold you up! Lay aside your own labors, give up your own struggle and resistance. Submit to God and say, "Let the waters of God hold me up."

You need to release the river of God within you. Just say, "I am bringing my tributary to the place of the tabernacles of God, and I'm going to let my river flow in." When you lift your hands to present the sweet incense of praise and prayer to God, you are also releasing the living river of God within you. Anyone else who comes along will also want to drink!

The river of God is identified by the trees that flourish on either side of it regardless of the year or season. We are the trees of God that Ezekiel saw on both sides of the river in the city of God. Our leaves are ordained for the healing of the nations! If you are planted by the river of life, then God will let you touch somebody, and healing will come forth out of you. Your leaves will never whither, even during the time of your persecution, tribulation, and trouble. Nor will they whither in the good season. Whatsoever you do will prosper.

One thing have I desired of the Lord, that will I seek after; that I may dwell in the house of the Lord all the days of my life, to behold the beauty of the Lord, and to inquire in His temple. For **in the time of trouble** *He*

*shall hide me in His pavilion: in the secret of His tab-
ernacle shall He hide me; He shall set me up upon a
rock. And now shall mine head be lifted up above mine
enemies round about me: therefore will I offer in His
tabernacle sacrifices of joy; I will sing, yea, I will sing
praises unto the Lord* (Psalm 27:4-6).

"In the time of trouble...." Sometimes troubles come one
at a time or in seemingly manageable pairs. Then there are
"times of trouble." That is when you desperately want God to
hide you in His pavilion in the "secret of His tabernacle." The
psalmist says, "He shall set me upon a rock" (Ps. 27:4). Our
Rock is a stable place, a fortress of strength that will never
fail. In times of trouble, God will give you a word that you
can stand on.

The Shout of Victory Will Arise

*And now shall mine head be lifted up above mine ene-
mies round about me: therefore will I offer in His tabernacle sacrifices of joy; I will sing, yea, I will sing
praises unto the Lord* (Psalm 27:6).

He lifts up our head and we will *zamar*, or "make music
and celebrate with praises," unto the Lord. God is out to turn
our crying into rejoicing, and He does this by planting our feet
on the Solid Rock right in front of our enemies and circumstances. When our feet become planted in the midst of great
storms and testing, you should begin to smell the fragrance of
victory, of soon-coming rain. It is almost time to move on to
the next level of God's glory!

In the Book of Revelation, Jesus told John, "He that hath
an ear, let him hear what the Spirit saith unto the churches; To

him that overcometh will I give to eat of the hidden manna, and will give him a white stone, and in the stone a new name written, which no man knoweth saving he that receiveth it" (Rev. 2:17). To overcome means that you passed through the fire of testing with victory. A white stone was given to somebody who had committed a crime like murder as a visible sign, or symbol, of acquittal. When a deal was cut or verdict declared, the accused was cut, as in a covenant, and was pardoned. Then he was given a white stone, a white camel, and a white tent. He then rode the white camel, lived in the white tent, and put the white stone in front of the tent to show that he was pardoned.

In ancient Greece, a white stone was given to winners in the early Olympic games. And it was a seal certifying to all that its possessor was a winner and that he had redemptive rights. His name was put inside the stone. You too have received an executive pardon and will receive a white stone if you persevere through the fire and walk in the victory of Jesus Christ. Best of all, our God declared, "To him that overcometh will I give to eat of the tree of life..." (Rev. 2:7b).

Chapter 10

When You Feel Like Quitting

There was a time in my life when I was desperately ill with what the doctors described as a terminal disease. I was running a fever and suffering so much pain that I began to think it would be easier for me to just go ahead and die rather than live. I was hurting so bad that I said, "God, just take me out of here."

Pressure Is Part of the Process

Then something rose up within to revive me. A voice told me, "You're not finished yet. You haven't kept the faith. You haven't fought a good fight yet. You're just suffering a little pain." I considered this then responded, "You're right." Sometimes we think that just because we're in pain that the battle is over. God says, "You are just in a little pain—but you're not done yet; you haven't even found your course yet; How can you think about quitting?" At that moment God will stretch out His right hand and revive you (as He did for me).

...If so be that we suffer with Him, that we may be also glorified together. For I reckon that the sufferings of this present time are not worthy to be compared with the glory which shall be revealed in us (Romans 8:17-18).

If the pressure is on you right now and you don't understand it, then you probably also don't know how to deal with it. Your first impression or urge when pressure comes will be to quit. "Praise the Lord" is the last thing you will want to say. But that is because you don't understand the purpose of God in the suffering, tribulation, and persecution that comes our way in life.

Once you understand God's purpose, you will understand that these things are simply "part of the package" of life. Sweat is part of the package of hard work, and when you become a Christian, God doesn't pull you out of the normal life cycles or put you in some cocoon after stamping "Exempt" across your forehead! There are certain things that simply will not come forth without some degree of pressure from persecution, suffering, and tribulation. Paul said something very peculiar about these challenges:

*So that we ourselves glory in you in the churches of God for your patience and faith in all your persecutions and tribulations that ye endure: which is **a manifest token** of the righteous judgment of God, that ye may be counted worthy of the kingdom of God, for which ye also suffer* (2 Thessalonians 1:4-5).

If you don't have something to compare with your suffering, then you will be tempted to quit when the going gets tough. But if you understand what God has placed in you and what He wants to *bring forth* in you, then you will say, "Do whatever it takes, Lord." You will say, "I have seen that what I will receive can't even be compared with the minor pain of the process." The point is: *Never confuse the process with the end.*

Pressure Comes With Promise

If I told you that today I had placed a bag with a million dollars near a highway intersection for you to pick up, then you would have a good picture of the reward waiting for you at the end of your hunt for this bag. No matter how long it might take for you to get there, it would still be waiting for you. Obstacles standing in the way would suddenly shrink before the vivid picture of the reward waiting for you. If you had no car, then you would borrow or buy one to get to the bag.

God has made a promise to you about something that is waiting for you in the end. You will have to "walk" to reach that end. You might say, "I know I'll get blisters on my feet, but once I get that million I'll go hire myself a foot doctor!" Don't ever confuse the end with the process. The suffering, the pressure, and the tension will always be waiting for before you reach the end. That is the time to simply press in! Don't despair—resistance is just part of the process. God says, "This is what it will take to birth you through." When circumstances go crazy, and everything looks like it's raising itself up against the knowledge of God, God says, "Keep on walking. Keep on casting down vain imaginations. Bring every thought into captivity. Stretch yourself out there in that faith and keep pushing."

When we yield to the temptation during suffering to ask, "Why?" we are saying, "God, explain this process to me."

Instead of asking why, I've learned to ask, "What is Your purpose in this, Lord? I know what I'm going through, and I don't need an explanation of the process. But would You please tell me what Your purpose is in this situation?"

Find the Purpose for Your Process

God invariably answers, "I want to reveal more of Myself in you." Once I understand the purpose and the end result of my suffering, I can say, "This ain't nothing. I'll just keep on going." A clear vision of the reward lets me know that if I would just walk it out, the reward would be there when I passed through the fire.

When you know what the end is, then your enemies and circumstances can toss you into a lions' den; yet you will still say, "Oh, this isn't anything compared to the good things awaiting me!" They can stoke up the fiery furnace as they did for the three Hebrew men in the Book of Daniel. They can take you down to the dungeon and say, "We're going to crucify you," but like Jesus who "for the joy that was set before Him endured the cross" (see Heb. 12:2), you will say, "This momentary affliction is nothing. It's just a process. Put me on that tree, and I'll be back in your face in three days with heavenly gifts in my hands!"

You won't mind going to the cross if you know that all you have to do is to count: "One, two, three!" The crucifixion was just the process. The resurrection, the new life, the redeemed Body of believers, the triumph over sin and death, the millions or billions of transformed lives, the glory given to the Father—*that* was the glorious end! This is why our present sufferings are not worthy to be compared to the things that

God wants to reveal in us. This is why He is so determined to shake everything that can be shaken so that "those things which cannot be shaken can remain" (Heb. 12:27).

Your Long-Awaited Arrival

The earnest expectation of all creation awaits the *manifestation of the sons of God* (see Rom. 8:19). All creation is waiting for you and I to come forth in God's glory. The Scriptures say that creation itself also "...shall be delivered from the bondage of corruption into the glorious liberty of the children of God" (Rom. 8:21). God wants to bring us all into a glorious liberty, and the whole creation is groaning in anticipation of our appearing!

God put us here for a purpose as part of His creation, but He created us in His own image to become His dwelling place, and His righteous sons and daughters. Immersed in His grand plan of redemption and glory, we have been transformed and made fertile with the love of God. All creation watches with expectancy and in anticipation of the day God will redeem it. Destroyed once by water, God has reserved creation again for purification by fire to receive His glorious Son. The earth is groaning, "I'm ready." The plants are breathing the same message. The faults of the earth's structure are moving. Volcanoes are exploding, groaning and yearning for the manifested sons of God to come forth.

We too are groaning for a new existence on a new level:

And not only they, but ourselves also, which have the firstfruits of the Spirit, even we ourselves groan within ourselves, waiting for the adoption, to wit, the redemption of our body (Romans 8:23).

Jesus Wants to Reveal Himself in You

It is almost as if we are "pregnant" with the manifestation of the Son of God inside of us. The image of Jesus Christ has been planted as a seed within our hearts. This divine seed in us has caused us to "grow up" from babes in Jesus to children in the temple. He's helped us grow up to the "young man" stage, and then to become fathers. Now He is growing us into a "perfect man" so He can be fully manifested in us as a "Glorified Man."

Jesus wants to come forth and reveal Himself in you. That is why your corporate body is going through such shaking and pressure. This is why every attitude is going through the fire of examination and purification. God says, "I must displace the fleshly and carnal so that My thoughts can reside in you. I will bring these things to death and life may take its place in you." Carnality naturally dies when it is "starved out" through fasting and prayer, and through the flesh-crucifying processes of persecution, tribulation, and suffering.

When we refuse to fast and pray to put certain things to death that are outside of God's best for us, our heavenly Father permits the pressure to come. When we complain, "But God this is killing me," He may reply, "I know. But it is all right. Haven't you read, 'Precious in the sight of the Lord is the death of His saints'?" (Ps. 116:15) The wise don't resist dying, they yield to it. Whenever God cuts off a portion of our lives or weakness, He always returns abundant life to replace the death He has removed from our lives. It is better to "lose an eye" (or a habit) than a life. God loves you enough to perfect you at any cost.

Verily, verily, I say unto you, Except a corn of wheat fall into the ground and die, it abideth alone: but if it die, it bringeth forth much fruit. He that loveth his life shall lose it; and he that hateth his life in this world shall keep it unto life eternal (John 12:24-25).

The Spirit Intercedes for Us

Sometimes we begin to say, "God, I know that there's more to this thing than what we're experiencing." Romans 8:24 says, "For we are saved by hope: but hope that is seen is not hope: for what a man seeth, why doth he yet hope for?" We are saved by hope. Hope is the vision of expectation for favorable change. Hope is the understanding that things won't remain the way they are.

But if we hope for that we see not, then do we with patience wait for it. Likewise the Spirit also helpeth our infirmities: for we know not what we should pray for as we ought: but the Spirit itself maketh intercession for us with groanings which cannot be uttered (Romans 8:25-26).

Not only does all creation groan with us, but the Spirit also groans in perfect prayer to help us in our weakness and infirmity "...with groanings that cannot be uttered." We are never weaker than when we are in the depths of a trial that shakes us to our very soul. In that moment when prayer is so desperately needed, we are usually helpless to pray effectively in our own strength, discernment, and wisdom. How does the Spirit help us?

Your Heart Is Open to Him

"And He that searcheth the hearts knoweth what is the mind of the Spirit, because He maketh intercession for the saints according to the will of God" (Rom. 8:27). This single passage describes two of the most vital functions of the Holy Spirit in our lives. First, God the Father knows everything that is on the mind of the Holy Spirit. The Father knows exactly how we feel and what we are thinking at all times. Nothing is hidden from Him. The Spirit continually intercedes for you and me. This is the first great function of the Holy Spirit. The second makes the first even more powerful. The Spirit prays for us "according to the will of God." That means His prayers are always answered, for they are in perfect unity with the mind and will of God the Father.

God searches the heart. He asks questions to make us seek answers (He already knows the truth): "What are your motives? Why are you doing this? What is your reasoning? Is it for the glory of My Son who shall be revealed in you, or is it for your own promotion? Is it for your own name's sake? Is it for your own reputation?"

This proving process permits the heat and pressure to try the value of the inner man. God highlights our impure motives, and says, "I need to burn off the chaff. I have baptized with the Holy Ghost—*and with fire!*" God's blessing always travels hand in hand with His character and His holiness. His fan is in His hand to thoroughly purge us of every impurity and unnecessary encumbrance (see Lk. 3:17).

He Knows What You Need

The Holy Spirit also intercedes on our behalf. Sometimes we don't even know what we're praying for. We label things brought on by the loving hand of God as the "work of the devil," and we label other things that are really from the devil as being the blessings of God. We don't whether to rebuke, bind, or welcome. That is why Jesus sent the Holy Spirit to "come alongside" and pray perfectly on our behalf.

We may be offering God unending "help me" prayers, "deliver me" prayers, and desperate "Lord, get me out of this" prayers. However when we finally begin to pray in the Spirit, He takes over and begins intercede perfectly for us, with us, and through us—and in perfect unity with God's will. Whether we pray in unknown tongues or with our understanding, when our prayer is empowered and guided by the Spirit, we pray in *harmonechia,* or harmony.

The Holy Spirit unfailingly finds the will of God in the midst of every situation, and He prays perfectly to that end. Whether our prayer effort finds us "out of season," or even wrong or misdirected, the Spirit of God says, "Let Me help your weaknesses. I know that you are flesh, and I know your limitations. You are finite, not infinite. You sometimes have a *word* of knowledge, but you do not *all* knowledge. You have a *word* of wisdom, not *all* wisdom. You may not know what to pray for, but I will pray the perfect will of God for you. I will make intercession according to the will of God so you can be stable and not run back and forth all the time."

His Plan Fits Everything Together

It is only with the understanding of the deep work of the Spirit on our behalf that we can properly declare the truth in Romans 8:28: "And we know that all things work together for good to them that love God, to them who are the called according to His purpose." If you say, "Well, God, this thing is ripping apart everything that I know and understand." He will say, "That is all right. There is a glory being revealed." When you begin to see what is being revealed inside you, you will say, "It's working together for the good. I didn't understand it when I was going through it. I didn't understand it when I was feeling it. But now I see it working together for good. I love you, Father. I understand Your purpose."

Once you understand the end result, you can begin to see how everything fits together. It will change your perception of your circumstances. "Why should I complain about a little bit of hurt and pain? It's just part of the process God is using to conform me to Christ's image. Displacement, continuous attitude adjustments, and battles with lusts of the flesh are just part of the birthing process God uses to reveal His Son in me."

To Be Glorified With Him

For whom He did foreknow, He also did predestinate to be conformed to the image of His Son, that He might be the firstborn among many brethren. Moreover whom He did predestinate, them He also called: and whom He called, them He also justified: and whom He justified, them He also glorified (Romans 8:29-30).

God wants to be glorified inside of us. He wants His Word to be revealed inside of us. Paul wrote to the Corinthians, "Blessed be God, even the Father of our Lord Jesus Christ, the Father of mercies, and the *God of all comfort*" (2 Cor. 1:3). The Greek root word for the term translated as "comfort" in this verse means "to come along side and strengthen." The next verse uses this term again in two forms: "Who *comforteth* us in all our tribulation, that we may be able to comfort them which are in any trouble, by the *comfort* wherewith we ourselves are comforted of God" (2 Cor. 1:4).

Comforted to Comfort

This Greek term for "comfort" is the same word used for the Comforter, the Holy Spirit. The word *parakaleo*, means "to call along side of." It is the root for the word *paracleat*, the name of the Holy Spirit. The Holy Spirit comforts us so that we can comfort others who are in trouble. It is difficult to comfort someone in grief if you've never experienced grief yourself. It is tough to comfort someone facing bitter disappointment if you have never experienced deep disappointment yourself.

For as the sufferings of Christ abound in us, so our consolation [our ministry, our consoling] *also aboundeth by Christ. And whether we be afflicted, it is for your consolation and salvation, which is effectual in the enduring of the same sufferings which we also suffer: or whether we be comforted, it is for your consolation and salvation. And our hope of you is stedfast, knowing, that as ye are partakers of the sufferings, so shall ye be also of the consolation* (2 Corinthians 1:5-7).

When Paul says "...whether we be afflicted it is for your consolation and salvation, which is effectual," he is saying his consolation to others is "effective" because of his suffering for Christ. You'll never be a consoler until you have been a partaker of sufferings.

Deliverance by Design

Paul said, "For we would not, brethren, have you ignorant of our trouble which came to us..." (2 Cor. 1:8). If most of us knew from the beginning that the Christian life included persecution, tribulation, and suffering— and if God gave us a choice of facing it or avoiding it—we'd never put in on the agenda. "Should I pray for suffering, persecution, tribulation?" No, God has already declared through Paul, "Yea, and all that will live godly in Christ Jesus shall suffer persecution" (2 Tim. 3:12). Therefore He's designed it to come to you. It will find you where you are, whatever you are doing. God knew that if it was up to us to pray for suffering or to schedule it on our agenda, we'd say, "No way."

Paul said he was pressed "out of measure" and beyond his own strength to the point where he even despaired for his life (see 2 Cor. 1:8). The pressure can be tough, but you and I must endure. Don't give up! When the pressure becomes so bad that you wonder if you will make it, that is the time to press in!

*...We should not trust in ourselves, but in God which raiseth the dead: who **delivered** us from so great a death, and **doth deliver**: in whom we trust that He **will yet deliver** us* (2 Corinthians 1:9-10).

Paul declares the answer to his dilemma in clear terms. We need to put our trust in God, who has delivered in the past, who is delivering us right now, and who will deliver us in the future without fail! In other words, wherever you are, God is your deliverer right now.

Regardless of what is out there in your tomorrow, you don't have to worry, because you can trust in the One who has delivered you in the past. You can remember when He paid your bill and healed your body. Remember when He saved you. He is the same yesterday, today, and forever (Heb. 13:8). If you want to understand what God is doing now and what

He will do tomorrow, find out what He did yesterday! You have a foundation for knowing what God will do in the future, but you need to know about your God before you get hit with pressure and trials.

The psalmist said in Psalm 46:1, "God is our refuge and strength, a very present help in trouble." By this he was declaring, "When my trouble hit, I didn't have to find my God. I located my God long before trials came my way." That is the key to victory for you and me.

Chapter 11

The Role of Fathers With Sons and Daughters

The Parent Principle

When I was a young Christian everyone told me to read the Bible, but no one ever *showed* me how to do it. Finally I told the Lord, "God, I need to understand how to read this Word." When God hears this kind of prayer, He responds in a very predictable way because He has laid down a pattern in His Word. He always sends spiritual fathers and mothers to spiritual children who need guidance, training, and discipleship. This principle of "parenthood" applies to every level of our growth from infancy to the "Glorified Man" in Christ.

Practical Preparation

Shortly after I prayed this prayer, to God, I met an older man who was seasoned in the faith. I felt a call of God on my life to preach, so I went to this man and said, "I feel like I've been called of God to preach." He asked me, "Have you been to Bible school?" I said, "Not yet." Then he asked me, "Do you know the Word of God?" I responded, "Well, I have read through the Bible...." Not satisfied, he asked, "Have you read *all the way through* the Bible?"

I ducked my head in shame. I was embarrassed to admit that I was getting ready to start preaching before I had even read all the way through the Bible. I explained to the man, "Every year, I make up my mind to read the Bible. I get one of those Bible lists and make a commitment to read through the Bible a little every day. Now in January I always do real well. I get through Genesis, Exodus, Leviticus, and Deuteronomy. But by the time I get over there to Samuel, Chronicles, and Kings, I run into those long lists of names and references to guys I know nothing about. I don't even know how to pronounce their names! I get so frustrated I just end up quitting most of the time."

This wise man said, "Brother, the reason you can't get through the Bible is that you're *reading it too slow*." He looked at me and said, "Brother, do this: Go home and buy yourself a large-print Bible—not a reference Bible, just a large-print Bible. Now the average large-print Bible has about 1,500 pages in it. I want you to read 15 pages a day."

He continued, "Start out in Genesis and read 15 pages the first day and put a book mark right where you stop reading. The next day, go 15 pages and put a book mark there. In 100 days you'll be through the Bible! That puts you through the Bible about three times a year, just by reading 15 pages a day. You'll be able to understand the principles of the Bible better, and all the pieces will begin to come together for you."

"Now if you take a year to read the Bible," he said, "you'll end up reading the Law in the Book of Leviticus, along with the Books of Deuteronomy and Joshua early in the year. Yes, you will learn the principles in those books, but by the time November rolls around and you begin reading the Book of Hebrews, you will try to reflect back on the Law from your reading at the first of the year and say, 'Well, I *think* I remember who Jethro was...didn't he have something to do with the priesthood?' "

He explained, "That spreads it all out over too long of a time and distance. But if you will take this Bible and go through it every 100 days, then it will become a living word to you. You will see this Book imprinted upon your heart."

I followed this man's advice for several years, and I began to see the Bible come together. It became a living epistle inside of me. I read the Bible all the way through apart from my Bible study time and meditation. Paul said, "Till I come, give attendance to reading, to exhortation, to doctrine" (1 Tim. 4:13). I gave myself to reading the Word, and it made a difference. Most folks misinterpret the Word because they don't first *read* the Bible. If you don't know what God's Word says, how can you understand what it means?

Building Upon the Foundation

Then I met another seasoned man of God who asked me, "LaFayette, how have you been reading the Bible?" I told him about my 15-page-a-day system, and he said, "Well, you should also read the New Testament—but five chapters at a time. Read the same five chapters through each day for an entire month. The Book of Ephesians has six chapters, so you can read three chapters in the morning and three chapters at night for 30 days. I know you're a preacher now, but read it." He told me, "If you use the same Bible version and you do this for 30 days, then at the end of that 30 days, you'll know the Book of Ephesians!"

Even if you're "ignorant," after a while something will work its way into you if it's repeated enough. This godly man said, "Just begin to read repetitiously through the Word. After you finish Ephesians, you should go to a longer book like Matthew. Spend four months in that gospel, assigning the first seven chapters to the first month, the second seven chapters to the second month, and so on. Read three chapters in the morning and the other four chapters at night. After four months, you will know the Book of Matthew"

"By swinging back and forth between the small and large books of the New Testament, you will complete your reading in about three years," he said. "But when you have finished, you'll know the New Testament. It will be planted down inside of you."

I am a slow reader, and at that time, I read a lot slower than I do today, but I began to read and study the Word of God the way this man had advised me. I started to see the Word of God planted down inside of me. I used to be a "concordance cripple." I was the preacher, but every time I wanted to find a verse I had to flip back to the back of my Bible to find the reference!

When I began to read the Bible on this man's "30-day plan," I began to remember key scripture verses and their exact location in the Bible. After 30 passes, your mind "takes a picture" of each passage. You even begin to "see" them in context! "Oh yeah, I know that one. It's on the right hand page, left column, halfway down."

In time, I could remember the contents of each of the major books. I could tell you that in John chapter one, Jesus said, "I am the light." In John chapter two, Jesus met a woman in Canaan and turned the water into wine. In chapter three, we find Nicodemus. In chapter four, Jesus meets the woman at the well.... I can tell you how you see the manifestation of Christ all the way through John. I can quote these things because I've read each of them 30 times for months at a time, not because I'm especially smart.

Begin With the Word

I tell young believers who are hungry for God's Word, "I want that Word down inside of you. If you do nothing else, I want you to wake up early in the morning and read the Word of God. Before long, I know I will see those "babes in Christ" begin to move to the next level." People need the Word of God inside of them. There is simply no substitute.

If I read the Word, then when I come to my friends in the faith, I can exhort them in the Word instead of giving them some worthless "piece of my mind" or words of criticism. God is calling us to speak the Word, but we can't speak the Word unless we understand the Word. I have discovered that if I put the Word of God inside the people and have them take responsibility for it, then they will begin to grow in the things of God.

Responsible Parenting

Paul wrote in Galatians 4:1, "Now I say, That the heir, as long as he is a child, differeth nothing from a servant, though he be lord of all." The word "child" is translated from the Greek word, *nepios*, which refers to a non-speaking infant. This Greek word is also translated as "babes"in First Peter 2. Every "babe" needs to be put under tutors and governors (most often its own "parents"). Babes in Christ shouldn't be running around trying to establish their ministries and run things while they are still in diapers.

Babes don't advance to maturity merely by growing older or through longevity of attendance. They could be with you five or six years and still be babes. They could even be with you for 20 years and still be babes. Babes are to be put under tutors and governors until the time appointed by the fathers. A father knows when his "babes" have grown up, and when it is time for them to branch out and move upward. Paul said, "Now I say, That the heir, as long as he is a child, differeth nothing from a servant, though he be lord of all" (Gal. 4:1). If the heir (*coronomos,* the one who is going to inherit all things) is still a *nepios*, a baby or infant that cannot speak, then he has no higher rank or leadership privileges than a *dulous*, a servant—even though he will eventually be lord of all. Such a child is placed under the care and oversight of governors and tutors until the time appointed by the father.

Authority Follow Maturity

If you are a leader in the church, then you can't afford to let your sympathy for people direct your actions. Of course, you will see the potential in them, but if you know that a person isn't ready to go and assume leadership authority yet, then straighten your back and say, "It's not time to go. You need to stay with your father. You need to mature a bit more under his government. You need to stay with this tutor until the time appointed by your spiritual father."

Pastors tend to naturally join with the hearts of the people. I've learned to reach out to my people and embrace them very tightly as I tell them, "I want you to stay here. I want to tutor you and I want to be a government unto you. I want you to hear me say, 'This is my son, this day I have begotten you in the Lord. It's time for you to go forth.' " When you are able to say that as a father, then you can release people out into ministry with blessing and honor.

That puts a stop to people running off to start things with no foundation upon which to build. That kind of "halfway" ministry only gets lots of other people in trouble because these immature leaders have no foundation of God's Word inside of them because they didn't submit to the discipline of planting His Word within. Every time a "new wind of doctrine" blows in, these people get puffed up and blown away in pride or deception. They don't have any revelation, maturity, or authority structure. Since everyone has to build on a foundation of some kind, these people just build on the first and most appealing new thought that comes along.

If you see people suddenly leave one ministry and immediately start to teach some weird doctrine, it is because they didn't stay under their God-given tutors and governors until the time appointed by their fathers.

I write unto you, little children, because your sins are forgiven you for His name's sake. I write unto you, fathers, because ye have known Him that is from the beginning. I write unto you, young men, because ye have

overcome the wicked one. I write unto you, little children, because ye have known the Father. I have written
unto you, fathers, because ye have known Him that is
from the beginning. I have written unto you, young
men, because ye are strong, and the word of God
abideth in you, and ye have overcome the wicked one
(1 John 2:12-14).

Position and Practice

The Greek word John used for "children" is *technion*. It
refers to a little infants, children who are just beginning to
walk, or to half-grown boys or girls. They have learned the
basic lessons of learning the Word. They have begun to apply
God's Word, and they are starting to see a little growth. Now
it's time to let them know their sins have been forgiven, and to
teach them who they are in Christ. They begin to want to put
off the accuser of the brethren, and shake off the past history
at this stage.

Identity

John the apostle told the flock of God, "I write unto you
children because you know your sins are forgiven you." Once
children develop speech and begin to interact with their peers
and adults, they can understand the truth that "there is therefore now no condemnation to them which are in Christ Jesus"
(Rom. 8:1). As they begin to see their shortcomings and
faults, a desire is born to shake off the hurts and wounds of
condemnation. They want to know "who they are." That is the
time for a spiritual father to lead them to the Book of Ephesians where they discover the "positional truth" of "in Him, in
whom, and by whom...*in Christ*." They learn that they serve

the Lord Jesus Christ, and that everything in Christ is positional truth. Even the triune name of God as the Father, the Son, and the Holy Ghost is reflected in the name of the Lord Jesus Christ.

Lordship

Lord speaks of divinity, the Eternal God in the Old Testament. *Jesus* is the name of His humanity, and *Christ* speaks of the anointing. Each of the three titles or names, Lord Jesus Christ, has a positional purpose and meaning. When "Lord Jesus" is used, it means the Father is working through His son. Sometimes you will see "Jesus Christ" used in Scripture. That is a picture of the Son anointed by or submitted to the Spirit. At other times you will see "Christ Jesus" used. That is a picture of the Spirit flowing through the Son. Then you may see all the fullness of the godhead revealed bodily when the full term, *Lord Jesus Christ,* is used. Even the titles and names of our Savior reveal and declare positional truth in the Kingdom of God.

God wants our position to line up with our practice, just as it did in the life of our Savior. We have each been blessed with "all spiritual blessings" in Christ, but we can still be (and often are) a mess. Yet in Heaven and the spirit realm, God sees us even the best of us (apart from Christ) as dung. Yes, you are blessed with all spiritual blessings, you are redeemed and glorified already, but that is all "in Christ," it is positional.

What does Jesus say? He describes the "position" that triggers the truth: "And why call ye Me, Lord, Lord, and do not the things which I say?" (Lk. 6:46) When you come under the government of God, He expects you to produce the "works" and "fruit" of obedience along with faith in your positional truth. We are exhorted by Paul the apostle:

*Wherefore, my beloved, as ye have always obeyed, not as in my presence only, but now much more in my absence, **work out your own salvation with fear and trembling.** For it is God which worketh in you both to will and to do of His good pleasure. Do all things without murmurings and disputings: That ye may be blameless and harmless, the sons of God, without rebuke...* (Philippians 2:12-15).

It is in the "childhood" stage that you begin to understand the "lordship" Scriptures in Ephesians chapter four. This is where Paul deals with family relationships and lifestyle. (As physical and spiritual parents, it is also important for us to teach our children and our "children in the faith" who they are in Christ.)

Adoption

I love to teach positional truth. I love to teach young believers that they are predestined, conformed, elected, and justified *in Christ.* I love to teach them how and why the blood of Jesus is the basis for everything of importance in the New Covenant and in the Old.

I tell them about shepherds in the Old Testament who had a unique way of dealing with "orphans" in the flock, and with adult sheep whose young had been stillborn. On rare occasions, a dam (a female sheep) would die while giving birth to a healthy lamb. The sire (or father) of the lamb would usually reject it because there was no mother to nurture it.

The shepherd would look for another sheep whose lamb was stillborn. The only way the orphan lamb would be "adopted" by the new family was for the shepherd to separate the sheep long enough for him to retrieve the body of the stillborn lamb. The shepherd put the blood of the stillborn lamb into a basin and pour it over the little orphan lamb. When he presented the little orphan lamb to the sire and dam, they could only smell the familiar smell of their own offspring. It was through the blood of the dead lamb that the living lamb was given a new identity as a member of the family and received as their own. In the same way, the blood of the Sacrificed Lamb of God is the basis for everything that you are. We were orphans and alienated from God, but the blood of Jesus washed us and made us acceptable in the family of God. Are you washed in the blood of the Lamb?

"First Principles"

Spiritual "childhood" is the age of discovery when the most fundamental truths are absorbed to support a lifetime of advancement to higher stages of life in Christ. It is spiritual fathers and mothers who are responsible for teaching young believers the "ABC's" of the faith outlined in Hebrews 6:1-2, including repentance from dead works, faith toward God, doctrines of baptism, baptism in water, baptism into the Body of Christ by the Spirit, and baptism by Jesus Christ with the Spirit of power. (I teach these "first principles" in my church once a year because I know I have children in the faith who are still finding out who they are. They need to understand this great salvation God has won for them.)

...I write unto you, young men, because ye have overcome the wicked one...I have written unto you, young

men, because ye are strong, and the word of God abideth in you, and ye have overcome the wicked one (1 John 2:13-14).

The Moderating Influence of the Parent

Believers in the "young man" stage have an especially strong need for spiritual fathers. John the apostle devoted the next three verses of his Epistle to warning Christians in the "young man" stage about the dangers of loving the world and its passions. These persons need the stability and established foundations of fathers to help them control the unproven strength they've discovered, and to help them keep their zeal in the center of God's will.

> *For every one that useth milk is unskilful in the word of righteousness: for he is a babe. But strong meat belongeth to them that are of full age, even those who **by reason of use** have their senses exercised to discern both good and evil. Therefore leaving the principles of the doctrine of Christ, let us go on unto perfection…* (Hebrews 5:13– 6:1).

It is natural for children to want to grow up. Children who enter the next level as young adults in the faith don't need as much counseling because they've learned to accept some responsibility for themselves. The Word of God is abiding inside of them in growing measure, and they are now beginning to overcome the wicked one instead of being seduced and drawn away by various sins. Not only do they still love to hear the testimony of the victorious, but they are becoming "the testimony" themselves.

Growing Independence

Their discernment has increased "by reason of use," so they are more aware of the importance of relationships with other people. When they were babes, their "fathers" nurtured and protected them and monitored their relationships. But in the "young man" stage, they begin to look out for themselves. They begin to sever certain unhealthy relationships with unbelievers in obedience to the Word of God abiding in them. This is the fruit of maturity.

As we noted in the first chapter, believers in the "young man" stage want to know nine key things: (1) Who is the enemy? (2) What does the enemy have? (3) What can the enemy do? (4) Who is God? (5) What does God have? (6) What can God do? (7) Who am I? (8) What do I have? and (9) What can I do?

As young believers learn these nine lessons, they also discover the grace of God. I can usually identify believers in the "young man" stage by their increased sensitivity and "devil-consciousness." I don't run them off just because they are "seeing demons" everywhere. I don't get too alarmed just because I overhear them tell an especially talkative friend, "You've got a 'talking spirit,' " or someone who continually chews gum, "You've got a 'chewing spirit.' "

These people are revealing to me that they have just broken into a new level of maturity. They are more conscious of the enemy and the way he operates. They don't need to be shunned and labeled as "weird." They simply need a shepherd to guide them. "I understand where you are. Let me teach you some balance. Don't label everything as belonging to either the Spirit or to the devil—some stuff comes from us!

Sometimes, people do things just because they're ignorant or don't know any better."

I made an appointment to meet someone in the vestibule of the church one time, and he was late. As my frustration grew, I noticed someone wandering around toward the bathroom, then drifting back down to the other side of the basement. Finally I realized what had happened. I went up to him and said, "Man, where have you been?" He said, "I was trying to find the 'vestibule.' " I said, "I'm sorry, I should have told you to meet me in the hallway, right here by the door." (I had used an old Baptist word, "vestibule," and this man just didn't know what I was talking about. He didn't have a "wandering spirit," he was just lost.)

New Discernment

Believers in the "young man" stage begin to learn the difference between ignorance and rebellion through the impartation of the Word of God. Sometimes leaders have to look beyond what they are seeing and say, "They are just growing up in the faith." They have to minister to these young believers to help them grow them up in the faith.

It is important to remember that just because people "hear from God" does not mean that they are mature. Samuel was a just a child when he first heard the voice of the Lord. When he first heard God's voice, he said, "That sounds like Eli." (The voice of the Lord for spiritual children and babes will generally sound a lot like their spiritual father's in the beginning.)

Spiritual fathers have an awesome responsibility to "grow up" the new generation that is destined to crush the enemy's head. That is why I teach believers about the weapons of our warfare in the Word of God. I teach them that the first thing the Son of God said when He was confronted by the devil in the wilderness was, "It is written...." Then I tell them to "go and do likewise."

Delegated Authority

Revelation chapter 12 makes it clear that the devil knows his time is short, and he is working furiously to destroy everything that is good and holy. Yet God isn't "fighting demons and devils any more." No, He is raising up a generation of bold young believers who are armed with His Word and the blood of the Lamb. Instead of saying, "Archangel Michael, take care of that!" He is saying, "Church, take care of that!"

Psalm 149:9 says, "To execute upon them the judgment written: this honour have all His saints...." When a judge in a court writes out his judgment, he doesn't just read his opinion off the top of his head. He spends time in his private chambers carefully writing a judgment in line with established law and statutes decreed by the land. When he pronounces judgment on a convicted criminal, he says, "Bailiff, handcuff the prisoner and take him away." God is saying, "Church, I have pronounced judgment on the devil. Now *you* bind him up and get him out of here."

God's Mandate to Multiply

"I write unto you, fathers, because ye have known Him that is from the beginning" (1 Jn. 2:13). God is raising up a mighty "fatherhood" or parenthood of men and women who are anointed to *reproduce* themselves in the Kingdom. Paul said in First Corinthians 4:15, "For though ye have ten thousand instructors in Christ, yet have ye not many *fathers*: for in Christ Jesus I have begotten you through the gospel." Very few people will take the time to impart their own soul unto another. That is why there are very few "fathers" and "mothers" in the Church today.

The "fathers," the men and women God is raising up in the faith today, understand the eternal purposes of God. They understand the purpose of the Church and what God is doing in the Kingdom. They understand the Kingdom principles of submission and release. They even know how to release rebellious children as the father in released his "prodigal" son and received him back again as a much wiser and more appreciative son. Although they know such "prodigals" are likely to waste time and substance, they will never lose their inheritance because their inheritance is in their spiritual fathers, and especially in their heavenly Father.

Nurturing God's Children

Like the apostle Paul, these men and women will also display a "feminine side of the ministry" in their shepherd's heart for God's flock:

> *But we were gentle among you, even as a nurse cherisheth her children: so being affectionately desirous of you, we were willing to have imparted unto you, not the gospel of God only, but also our own souls, because ye were dear unto us. For ye remember, brethren, our labour and travail: for labouring night and day, because we would not be chargeable unto any of you, we preached unto you the gospel of God. Ye are witnesses, and God also, how holily and justly and unblameably we behaved ourselves among you that believe: as ye know how we exhorted and comforted and charged*

every one of you, as a father doth his children, that ye would walk worthy of God, who hath called you unto His kingdom and glory (1 Thessalonians 2:7-12).

Paul was saying, "We were like a nurse among you. We were gentle, tender, affectionate toward you. When we noticed that you had grown, we brought you out of the nursery and began to walk among you saying, 'This is the way you walk.' We began to charge and exhort you." The Greek word translated as "comforted" in this passage doesn't mean "do it for them," but to "come along side and help do it."

My wife is a great mother. She faithfully nurtures, instructs, and rescues our three children every day. But there comes a time where the father has to step in with the masculine side of child rearing. When she says, "I have to get something downstairs, but I'm too tired to go get it," I say, "You don't have to go downstairs—you have sons. Send those boys down there to pick it up for you. You have a daughter. God has given us two kings and a queen, two sons and a daughter." I tell my children that they are doing these things because God has predestined them to be kings in the earth. We speak these things into their lives because we're fathers. Fathers don't always "do things" for their children. They must also teach them to work and take responsibility for things.

Release to Responsibility

Raising children follows a natural path of increasing independence and responsibility. While a father may "do everything" for little children, the day will come when he will say, "Now, I want you to do it *with* me." Then comes the stage where he says, "I'm going to let you do it by yourself while I watch." Finally the father will tell his growing child, "You're out of here. You are going to do it all by yourself."

That is what Jesus did with His disciples. He said, "Follow Me." At first, Jesus did everything. Then He began to teach them and involved them in His ministry. When He fed the five thousand (Mt. 14:15-21), He didn't go out and personally hand bread and fish to 5,000 men and their families. No, He broke and consecrated the fish and loaves in prayer. Then He called His disciples and said, "You go feed the people and collect the fragments."

When He felt it was time to take the message of the Kingdom into other villages and cities, according to the account in Luke chapter 10, He sent His disciples ahead of Him by twos. He just "sent His sons" to do the job of preparing the way for Him. When they returned all excited because demons were subject to them in Jesus' name, He basically said, "I'm glad you found that out, but don't just rejoice about that. That was your 'young man' stage. I want you to grow you up. Be glad that your name is written in the Lamb's book of life" (see Lk. 10:20). Jesus adjusted their theology so they could begin to learn more about Him.

The Time for Training

Fathers know that they cannot minister to everybody on the same level all the time. Some have to follow "at a distance" while watching and learning. Some people in our church have told me, "I'm watching you." I responded, "I know. I want you to just follow." Later on, they came to me and said, "I want you to train me" (the popular word today is *mentor,* but the biblical word is *disciple*).

*Then said Jesus to those Jews which believed on Him,
If ye continue in My word, then are ye My disciples in-
deed; and ye shall know the truth, and the truth shall
make you free* (John 8:31-32).

Jesus told them, "Come unto Me and learn of Me" (see
Mt. 11:28-29). They obeyed, followed, and began to learn. Finally He was able to release them as fathers in the faith, and
they turned the world upside down. No one has a right to be
released from a father in the faith until the time appointed by
the father.

The prophet Elijah had a "father and son" relationship
with his younger protégé, Elisha, in the Book of Second
Kings. The younger man had left family and home to follow
and serve Elijah faithfully, and he knew his teacher was about
to taken to Heaven. He refused to leave his teacher, no matter
where he went or what he said. Finally, the old prophet turned
to Elisha and said:

*Ask what I shall do for thee, before I be taken away
from thee. And Elisha said, I pray thee, let a double
portion of thy spirit be upon me. And he said, Thou
hast asked a hard thing: nevertheless, if thou see me
when I am taken from thee, it shall be so unto thee; but
if not, it shall not be so* (2 Kings 2:9b-10).

That Hebrew word for "see" is *ra'ah*, and it means, "If
you can be eye-to-eye with me." He was saying in effect,
"When I go up, you will have not only what I gave you, but
you will have what I will leave you (because what I gave you
was not all you need)."

Elisha saw fiery chariots come by, and that was a great revelation in itself, but the double portion wouldn't come from them. He saw whirlwinds come, but he knew his blessing wasn't in the wind. No, this young spiritual son kept his eye on his spiritual father. He stayed "eye-to-eye" with Elijah. After the whirlwind and the fiery chariots came, Elijah rose up in the air—yet faithful Elisha stayed eye-to-eye with Elijah until the old prophet's mantle came down. The very first words Elisha says reveal exactly where his heart was. He didn't shout "Elijah, oh Elijah." He didn't say, "Prophet, oh prophet." No, he said in anguish, "My father, my father!" (2 Kings 2:12) Referring to Elijah as a type of the coming Messiah, Malachi declared, "and He shall turn the heart of the fathers to the children, and the heart of the children to their fathers, lest I [God] come and smite the earth with a curse" (Mal. 4:6).

Receive the Prodigal

I believe a flood of "prodigal sons" will be turning from their rebellion back to their spiritual fathers and mothers—as did Onesimus, the runaway slave for whom Paul intervened with Philemon:

> *I beseech thee for my son Onesimus, whom I have begotten in my bonds: which in time past was to thee unprofitable, but now profitable to thee and to me* (Philemon 1:10-11).

These wayward sons will come back and say, "I want to be trained. I was wrong. Can I just carry your coat or pour water over your hands?" Their fathers will end up taking them from Gilgal to Bethal, to Jericho, and finally over Jordan where they will impart to these sons and daughters what God has given to them. These fathers in the faith aren't interested in just "holding" their sons and daughters all their lives, they want to see them mature. Yet they must all stay under the tutors and governors until the proper time for them to become fathers and mothers themselves.

The Universal Body

The apostle Paul describes the next level facing fathers and mothers in the faith when he describes the role and goal of "equippers" in the Church, who are to help perfect the saints for the work of the ministry and build up the Body "till we all come in the unity of the faith, and of the knowledge of the Son of God, *unto a perfect man*, unto the measure of the stature of the fulness of Christ" (Eph. 4:13).

"Until we come unto the perfect man." At this level, fathers begin to take responsibility for other people. The Greek word Paul used for "perfect" was *teleios*. It speaks of completeness in full age, the perfect man. It means that the application, the labor, and the growth of the mental character has been developed. The stage of the "perfect man" involves men and women who are moving *together* as "fathers." They have not become isolated. They are not saying, "I'm a father in the faith, I don't need anybody." They understand that God wants us all to come into the unity of faith. Those in the stage of the "perfect man" have a desire to see the whole Body of Christ achieve it's full potential.

Corporate Responsibility

I'm not concerned merely with Rhema Christian Center in Columbus, Ohio. I am concerned with the "church Columbus," composed of many believers and "fathers." I also have a broad vision and an international camaraderie and "blood relationship" with the one true Church in the nations. I want to see God's Church universal rise up in glory and perfection. The "perfect man" understands responsibility for and to others.

The modern Church is beginning to experience the *corporate responsibility* revealed in the Old Covenant with the sin of Achan. When Israel suffered a terrible defeat at the hands of the tiny city Ai, God told Joshua, "There is an accursed thing in the midst of thee, O Israel: thou canst not stand before thine enemies, until ye take away the accursed thing from among you" (Josh. 7:13b). There was sin in the camp. The sin of one had brought failure to all. A man named Achan had broken the direct command of God and taken gold and clothing from among the spoils of Jericho. The same kind of things get us into trouble in our churches today. The central problem wasn't the sin itself; it was Achan's concealment of His secret sin. God was determined to reveal it and purify His people. God is out to reveal what we have concealed so that His people, His Church, His bride, will be pure and holy before Him.

Once we advance individually to a certain point, God takes us higher. The highest levels of obedience involve *corporate responsibility*. Paul told the Church that a little leaven will leaven (or corrupt) the whole lump (1 Cor. 5:6). Fathers taking the lead in the "perfect man" stage have begun to understand that "what I do effects you." In fact, what I do in Columbus, Ohio, will actually affect you—whether you are in San Diego, California; Atlanta, Georgia; in Detroit, Michigan; or in Buffalo, New York. I believe we are more connected by the Spirit than any of us realize. What you and I do affects one another. The "perfect man" is one who understands that God wants to bring us "all" to full age where we "all" blossom and mature together.

Perfected for the Father

I tell folks in our church, *You* don't have any business—it's the *Father's business* that we're interested in!" What do I mean by that? I'm just following the priority of Jesus, who told His earthly father and mother, "...Wist [know] ye not that I must be about My Father's business?" (Lk. 2:49b) We need to grow up into the "perfect man" *together*.

Hebrews 11 lists the people who were in the great "hall of fame of faith," and it closes with the statement, "God having provided some better thing for us, that they *without us* should not be made perfect" (Heb. 11:40). Did you know that you can't even be crucified with Christ by yourself? Oblige me for a moment for the sake of an important point: You may be able to nail your own feet to the cross. You may even manage to push the crown of thorns into your head, and hold the nail somehow so you can nail one hand down. Yet one hand will still be left free—someone will have to have to come along and nail the free hand down for you.

Sometimes God sends people into your life who will give you headaches, frustrations, and all kinds of character-building problems. Thanks to their "ministry," you will end up praying, "God, this is killing me!" He will simply say, "I know." Part of our perfection comes through the people God sends into our lives to help crucify the deadly things hidden in us. I just began to thank God for those people. Zechariah the prophet put it this way, "And one shall say unto him, What are these wounds in thine hands? Then he shall answer, Those with which I was wounded in the house of my friends" (Zech. 13:6). If your "free hand" of unrevealed sin or fault is still alive and running loose, God will most likely send along someone who is willing and able to crucify that loose sin.

There is always some saint (or fellow father) who will say, "I'll do it, God." We need each other to be perfected.

This is a crucial point to understand: Although your *talent* can be perfected through your individual work and obedience, your *character* can only be perfected as you live and work in the context of *other people.* Character is born and developed in the house of God. Some people stay away from certain places because they know that if thy let you get too close to them, you might see who they really are and what they are desperately hiding.

Covenant Accountability

God says, "If you are going to be perfected, you will have to get close to somebody. You must have someone near you who can ask crucial questions in your life about the three great temptations of the world: the lusts of the flesh, the lusts of the eye, and the pride of life." This only happens in covenant relationship—where we don't have a choice in the matter.

One brother sat in my office and said, "I want to be a minister." I told him, "These three are in the world, the lust of the flesh, lusts of the eye, and the pride of life. *Which one effects you?*" He looked offended as he said, "I don't have any of those." I told him, "I know what your problem is. You're dealing with the pride of life." We all need someone to sit us down and ask us the hard questions so we can go on to perfection together. We need someone who loves us enough to ask, "How are you treating your spouse? What is your bedroom life like? How are you handling your finances? How are you treating your children?" Accountability helps us all come into the unity of the spirit and the bond of peace and unto the "perfect man."

Chapter 12

Beholding Jesus in Every Level

At last we come to the "Glorified Man." In Romans 8:18, Paul wrote to the church at Rome, "For I reckon that the sufferings of this present time are not worthy to be compared with the glory which shall be revealed in us."

Glorified Together Through Him

For whom He did foreknow, He also did predestinate to be conformed to the image of His Son, that He might be the firstborn among many brethren. Moreover whom He did predestinate, them He also called: and whom He called, them He also justified: and whom He justified, them He also glorified (Romans 8:29-30).

God has glorified some, and He's bringing forth glory in others. How can I say that? The "Glorified Man" stage is a *finished* work in Christ. He already sees you there. The "Glorified Man" is also a *progressive* work because according the

Bible, we are *moving* from glory to glory right now: "...we all, with open face beholding as in a glass the glory of the Lord, are changed into the same image from glory to glory, even as by the Spirit of the Lord" (2 Cor. 3:18).

From Glory to Glory

Corporate responsibility is important in the Body of Christ. When I set an elder in place, I first make sure that the leader is moving toward that "perfect man." Not only must this individual be a proven "father in the faith," but I want to hear him speak words of corporate responsibility. When I hear people talking about "my ministry" and "what I've done," then I know they have not moved toward that "perfect man" stage because the fruit of the mouth is more concerned with "me, I, and mine" than with "we, us, and His."

The "Glorified Man" is in the "past tense." The Bible speaks of those whom He *has* called, justified, predestinated, and glorified. God sees you glorified already because he already sees your end before Him. The "Glorified Man" stage is also ongoing, and consistent. That also means it is a present work. I *was* glorified in Christ, I *am being* glorified progressively, and I *will be* glorified in Him.

God is moving you to the ultimate end of the "Glorified Man," and yet He says, "Even when you get to that end, you have not reached the end." The Bible says, "Unto Him be *glory in the church* by Christ Jesus throughout all ages, world without end" (Eph. 3:21). He is to receive glory upon glory upon glory throughout eternity. In the heavenlies and in the earth, as kings and priests before God, we will keep moving from glory to glory.

The Weight of Glory

This level of the "Glorified Man" is interesting. Paul told the Corinthians, "For our light affliction, which is but for a moment, worketh for us a far more exceeding and *eternal weight of glory"* (2 Cor. 4:17). I like to see people change in their "weight" of glory. The *doxa* (glory) speaks of the weight of a thing, of being loaded down with glory! It speaks of the dignity or company of a thing, to be glorious, holy, and full of honor. These are the characteristics of glory. God wants you to understand that He will glorify you, and lead you from glory to glory.

We are changed as we behold His face. You will get a different picture of Him every time you look at Him. One of my favorite ways to behold God is through His Word. Psalm 18 is a warfare song that presents a powerful series of "portraits" of God in His glory: "The Lord is my rock, and my fortress, and my deliverer; my God, my strength, in whom I will trust; my buckler, and the horn of my salvation, and my high tower" (Ps. 18:2).

Our Strength

This passage contains the fascinating phrase, "I will love Thee, O Lord, my strength" (Ps. 18:1b). As I started meditating on those words, I began to understand that God really is the strength of my life. "The Lord is my rock" (Ps. 18:2a). As I began to behold Him as my Rock, I realized I was being changed into that very image in glory! I used to be real slippery and unstable, but I beheld Him, received Him, and claimed Him as my Rock; and I was changed into a stable man.

I discovered that He was my fortress when storms started to hit my life. (Storms are not uncommon to this faith and to the way of Christ.) When the storms began to hit, I beheld my God as my fortress, only to discover that I was transformed into a fortress as well. When missiles come my way now, there is something in me that repels the devil's fiery darts even though I feel like I am dying at the same time! As I beheld Him, I discovered that I would not quit or step aside when hard times come. I am changed. I am determined to "go down with Him" if I have to, for I know I will come up again. How can I be so sure? I know that any death in Christ results in a resurrection. I have discovered that He is my fortress.

Our Deliverance

My God is my "deliverer." I found that when I became bound, entangled, and surrounded by people, circumstances, and even my own shortcomings and weaknesses, that God is my deliverer. Sometimes He has to deliver me from my own limitations, but in every situation, He is my deliverer. Again, I discovered that as I beheld Him as my deliverer, He transformed me into a deliverer for others in need.

My God, my strength, in whom I will trust; my buckler, and the horn of my salvation, and my high tower. I will call upon the Lord, who is worthy to be praised: so shall I be saved from mine enemies (Psalm 18:2b-3).

I've read these verses many times, and at each of those levels I have prayed, "God I want to know You in the power of Your resurrection. I want to know You in the fellowship of Your suffering. I want to be made conformable to You in death" I began to understand that I can be glorified from glory to glory.

Progressive Perfection

I can quickly identify people who are being glorified. They are men and women who understand and share a progressive view of who God is. Their personal experience with the Lord has become a progressive process of continual perfection and glorification. We just don't receive Him and then say, "I was born again. I was saved, sanctified, and filled with the Holy Ghost." No, we can no longer give a testimony like that as if God is limited to something that happened in 1977. We can tell you who God is to us today, right now

Right now, in the midst of my writing, I found Him in Isaiah 9:6: "For unto us a child is born, unto us a Son is given: and the government shall be upon His shoulder: and His name shall be called *Wonderful*...." That means that Jesus Christ is awesome. He is high and radiant. He is good. I looked up the Hebrew word for "wonder," and I discovered that there are 30 different synonyms for "wonderful"! The prophet Isaiah just says, "I can't tell them all to you, so I'll just have to express it with one word—*wonderful*."

When folks ask me how I'm doing, I say, "I'm wonderful! I'm changing into that same image in glory." Now if they asked me, "Is everything all right in your life?" I would have to say, "Everything isn't all right, but I'm wonderful because I have been with "Wonderful" Himself this morning. I am being changed. Even though my circumstance maybe the same, I am wonderful because I've been with Wonderful."

The Glory of His Presence

We need to move progressively with God so He can move us to the place of His glory. In the old covenant, the place of glory was called "the Most Holy Place." It was located in the innermost court of the tabernacle in the wilderness. The outer court contained the brazen altar and the laver. The second court, called the Holy Place, was accessible only by the priests, and it contained the golden candlestick or lampstand, the table of showbread, and the altar of incense. If you passed through the veil of the Holy Place, you would enter the Holy of Holies, or the Most Holy Place. There was the Ark of the Covenant. It was the realm of God's glory on the other side of the cross.

People who are entering the glorified realm understand that out in the "outer court" they meet Jesus as Savior, and as the water baptizer. In the middle realm, or Holy Place of the New Covenant, we meet Him as the one who baptizes us with the Holy Ghost. It is in this innermost court of His glory that we also meet Him as the baptizer with fire. This is where He purges His threshing floor and place of judgment. In the outer court, we meet Him as "The Way." But in the middle court, we meet Him as "The Truth," in the midst of the bread loaves and the candlestick of worship. Inside the place of glory, the Most Holy Place, we meet Him as "The Life."

Jesus, Christ, and Lord

These parallels are almost endless, but we must continue for a better understanding of the "Glorified Man." In the outer court of our experience in Christ, we meet Him as *Jesus*: "That at the name of Jesus, every knee shall bow … Thou shalt call His name Jesus: for He shall save His people from their sins" (Phil. 2:10; Mt. 1:21b). However, in the Holy Place, we meet Him as the *Christ*, "the anointing," the power of God. In the Most Holy Place, He is revealed in all His glory, and we meet him in His governmental authority: We meet Him as *Lord*.

In the outer court, we meet Him at Passover as our Passover lamb, who was sacrificed for us. In the middle court, we meet Him at Pentecost, where He pours His Spirit out upon us and fill us up to overflowing in baptism. In the Most Holy Place, we meet Him as tabernacles (or "habitation, dwelling place, the indwelling God"). In the innermost court, we meet Him as the Lord of Hosts. This is His militant character as the God of expansion. He is the God who loves to come and take over. He doesn't take sides; He just takes over.

Faith, Hope, and Love

Paul summed up his detailed discussion of the Church and spiritual gifts with an amazing statement: "And now abideth faith, hope, charity [love], these three" (1 Cor. 13:13a). In the outer court, we met Him as Faith. In the second court, the Holy Place, we met Him as Hope. But in the Most Holy Place, in the innermost sanctuary, we met Him as Love.

Thanksgiving, Praise, and Worship

In the outer court of our beginnings as Christians, everything is brazen (or brass). In the next stage, the Holy Place, everything is silver. In the Most Holy Place, everything is gold. Out in the outer court, we met Him as "30-fold" Christians with a strong understanding of our salvation. In the Holy Place, we met Him as "60-fold" Christians with increased knowledge of His Word, the baptism of His Spirit, and increased fruitfulness. Praise God, there are some who are destined to step over into a place of glory where they will meet Him as "100-fold" Christians! Remember the writings of the apostles, the early church *fathers*: I write unto you *children* (in the outer court), I write unto you *young men* (in the Holy Place of kingship and the priesthood), and I write unto you *fathers* in the Most Holy Place.

In the outer court, we meet Him in an attitude of thanksgiving. We still enter into His gates with thanksgiving in our hearts. Yet in the Holy Place, we move a step higher and enter into His courts with praise. But once we step beyond the veil in the Most Holy Place, we not only bless His name and offer thanks to Him, but we begin to worship Him adore Him from the depths of our beings in spiritual worship.

As the veil drops and the gates slam, we stand before Him enraptured in love, adoration, and celebration of the Beloved. We are fascinated by Him. It is in the Most Holy Place that the picture of the Bride and the Bridegroom most appropriately match spiritual reality. Here in His presence, as we love Him with all our hearts and all our strength, in the midst of our love-making in worship our Maker plants a divine seed inside of us, the seed of His Son. Our spirits become pregnant with the seed of His Son. Suddenly we begin to understand that we were not called as a bride simply to walk at His side and "be seen." No, this Husband wants to form a Son inside of us!

We return from that intimate experience pregnant with a new revelation of the Son within us, and we begin to understand just who He is. Isaiah tells us out that in the outer court, you meet Him as the judge. But He is also the lawgiver in the middle court. Now we have met Him as the King who is moving us from glory to glory.

The outer court can be compared to the first 1,000 years of the Church. The middle court, the Holy Place, is the second 1,000 years of the Church, and it is coming to an end. Now we're getting ready to go into the third 1,000 years of the Church, and remember: "One day is with the Lord as a thousand years, and a thousand years as one day" (2 Pet. 3:8b).

In the "church of the first day," Jesus said, "I cast out devils, and I do cures to day and to morrow, and the third day I shall be perfected" (Lk. 13:32b).

Enter and Abide

In one of the countless parallel passages in the Old Testament, Joshua warned the Israelites to prepare food because in three days, they would cross over Jordan and possess the promised land (Josh. 1:11). God is bringing forth a "third day" Church that is full of glory and power. This isn't just a "one-man show," it is a Church filled with people who have been in the presence of God and have basked in His glory. They have learned not only how to ascend unto His presence, but how to abide in His glory as well.

The psalmist asked, "Who shall ascend into the hill of the Lord?" (Ps. 24:3a) But he also mentions another group: "Lord, who shall abide in Thy tabernacle? who shall dwell in Thy holy hill?" (Ps. 15:1) The "Glorified Man" is not content to "run in and out" of the presence of God. He is the one who walks in the presence of God so closely that he doesn't have to "chase" demons. When he enters an area, the demons scream out, "Why did you come?!"

God has destined some to be glorified, and it is time for us to preach it loudly and clearly. God has destined a people to be glorified in the innermost court. All this time, He has been saying:

> "Children, I have desired for you to come on in to My abiding presence. Yes, you can stop at Passover if you choose, and simply celebrate your salvation from destruction and sin. You can even stop at Pentecost and be content with your baptism with the Holy Ghost. Yet there is a people who are destined to go on into the third day. They are destined for tabernacles, to abide forever in My presence."